Pi.

FROM THE WOMB OF SKY AND EAR⊺ᴎ

C&R PRESS 2022
NONFICTIOIN PRIZE WINNER

"Leslie Contreras Schwartz's nonfiction debut is a book of witness that refuses to look away. As Contreras Schwartz's stunning sentences wend their ways around personal trauma and motherhood, structural racism and misogyny, bodies ill and bodies sexualized, and legendary death lords and misunderstood miracle workers, we as readers also can't look away— it's that magnetic, electric, incantatory. Time and again, these essays uncover the secret shared spaces between the corporeal and the ecstatic, that which we inherit, and that which we must tear down to start anew. In lending such careful lyric attention to her subjects, Contreras Schwartz's essays become re-dedications of the so-called 'whole stories' of our world. This book is brilliant, beautiful, wrenching, and wholly badass."
– Matthew Gavin Frank, author of *Flight of the Diamond Smugglers*

"*From the Womb of Sky and Earth* is a tremendous memoir, exploring everything in the world with brutal honesty: motherhood, childhood, violence, the body, trauma, friendship, power. With gorgeous, evocative prose, Leslie Contreras

Schwartz shows how joy and darkness reside side by side. The is an extraordinary, necessary work about pain and the complexity of survival, a work of exploration and witness; read it now."
– Karen E. Bender, author of *Refund*, 2015 National Book Award finalist

"*From the Womb of Sky and Earth* is haunting and visceral. Contreras Schwartz wades into deeply personal water, drawing on cultural myths and histories to navigate recollections of harm and struggle. Through swells of memory, the prose reveals ways to do more than survive. *From the Womb of Sky and Earth* is about learning how not to be crushed by waves of indignity; how to preserve and exalt oneself."
– Donald Quist, author of *Harbors* and *To Those Bounded*

FROM THE WOMB OF SKY AND EARTH

LESLIE CONTRERAS SCHWARTZ

C&R Press
Conscious & Responsible
Winston-Salem, NC

FROM THE WOMB OF SKY AND EARTH

TABLE OF CONTENTS

In the beginning, the girl is not believed.

In the epic poem and sacred text of the Maya people, *The Popol Vuh*, the daughter of a death lord sees a delicious fruit hanging from a calabash tree. Like Eve, she sees the lime-green fruit and believes it is natural to be hungry for it, to want it, to take it.

Unbeknownst to her, the fruit is the living head of a mortal who was defeated by the death lords. But the girl is curious, even after the head speaks. When she speaks to the man's head, he suddenly spits in her hand, and the girl, whose name is Lady Blood, becomes pregnant with his seed.

But her father does not believe the story of how she came to be pregnant, and Lady Blood uses trickery and escapes to the Earth's surface to avoid being murdered by him. Once among mortals, Lady Blood is still not believed by her mother-in-law, the mother of the man who spit in her hand, and when she asks the mother-in-law for her help, she is rejected. It is only when she can perform a miracle—grow corn out of an empty field overnight—that she is taken seriously. She bears twin sons who become the heroes that venture into the underworld to defeat death and its false deities.

Just like their mother, the twins use trickery and magic to survive, and it is this activity of ingenuity that creates the universe as we know it, with its sun, moon, and stars, the Earth and its blue-green lake of a sky. As *The Popol Vuh* describes, all the world comes from "the measuring and staking, / the halving and stretching / of those cords that contain / the womb of sky and earth."

> So the four corners and four sides
> were laid out, as it is said,
>
> by the Framer and the Shaper,
> mother-father of life and birth,
> giver of breath, giver of heart
>
> those that bear the never-ending light,
> those who hearten the sunlit children …
>
> they are tender in all things,
> the Framer and the Shaper,
> the knowers of all things,
> all that there is in sky and earth and lake and sea.[1]

---

1   *The Popol Vuh: A New English Version.* Trans. Michael Bazzett. (Minneapolis, MN: Milkweed Editions, 2018), 4-5.

How Myth Makes Reality

My mother says I'm a liar, that I invent the hellscape of my childhood. When I remember her episodes of rage, even when I contextualize the leather belt, hair pulling across the house, my head pounding the wall or the floor, the force feedings, severe punishments for my superstitions and childhood fears. She was a young mother who was profoundly damaged by an abusive adoptive mother, a religious fanatic whose punishments seem horrifically tied to violence committed against indigenous peoples in Mexico by priests and nuns in Catholic missionaries. In recollection, every tantrum or fight with my sister, my cries as a baby, triggered a transformation of place from our home in Northwest Houston, its relative peace of a lower middleclass community of Mexican American and Black families, to the Maya Underworld, Xibalba, where my mother was Lady Blood, navigating a landscape where she was hunted by a death lord. One second my mom was the young mother breaking up sisters' squabbles over toys or television channels; the next she was a child spilling a glass of water, her mother, our Lita, roaring down the hallway of a 1940's bungalow in the Mexican neighborhood of North Houston. Lita reciting Hail Mary's in Spanish to exorcise the devil from her child body. My mother was not in our house but was an elementary school student in the 1950's, a girl who was not allowed to speak at her Catholic school—was forced to remain mute—was beaten in front of the classroom for not knowing English. She was a ten-year-old tied to a bed and prayed over and whipped by nuns and her mother for telling them her own uncle exposed himself to her in a closet. The curañdero rituals using an egg and crucifix to catch the spirit of the devil as it was beaten out of her body. When she pulled us by the hair across the house, threw us against the wall, we were not her children. We were her mother, the nun, her uncle, and she was fighting for her own life....

*

It stops here. My daughter is screaming and pounding the walls. A primal urge runs up my spine. I want to make it all stop. She's melting down for reasons I cannot figure out and for reasons she probably doesn't know either.

And now it is 2010 and my hand ready to hit my daughter is raised in the air.

She's five years old, or eight years old, or twelve years old.

She's hungry, or she's sleepy, she's had a stressful day at school, and I am the safest person with whom to express her anger and frustration. Her screams attack my senses, fill up the house.

And now, as my mind switches between worlds, my daughter's presence asserts itself to freeze time. Though my mind wants to shift between stories that exist in me, they are stories I can't let be passed on, stories for which I won't create fertile landscapes. I see my child and the moment skids, begins to freeze by my own will.

I want to cover my hands over my ears. I want to run outside. My mother is in the house and I'm running to the closet, hiding under the bed. I imagine grabbing her, shaking her, hitting her to make her stop. My daughter is my mother and I am my mother's mother, my daughter is Lita. Sometimes I get close to hurting my child in my mind, I wrap my arms around her, I grab her by the wrist and make her sit or try to calm her. I am angry, I yell, I cry. But never do I do to her even one thing close to what was done to me or my siblings when we behaved the same way as children.

My mind freezes and turns off the light of my childhood. Pulls the shades and rejects the things my mother did and would do still. Never. From some inner source I conjure up, I learn how to help my daughter, how to help myself. I learn how to be peaceful when the house and my children and my husband are angry, or sad, or frustrated.

So, I don't. I don't transform to Lita, I don't transform into my mother. And I don't do the things that my mother did to her own children when she could not bear our existence: I do not grab my daughter by the hair and drag her outside, to the front yard, or to the backyard, or to the bathroom. I do not beat her with my fists, or a leather belt, or a brush, or a broom. I do not throw her against the wall, or pound the screams out of her body.

I don't force her into a bathtub of scalding water. I don't put her into a wagon and roll the wagon into the middle of the street.

I don't throw her clothes out onto the lawn. I don't grab a handful of clothes, stuff it into a backpack, force her into the car, and drop her off on a bridge. All of these actions, and worse, I never do because the trauma lives still in my body, down to the root of my neck and spine and I don't want my child to inherit what I carry. Every day I work to exorcise my childhood from my being. It will not hurt my child, and, later, my other two children.

*

I am not perfect. I scream or give bear hugs to prevent the child from hurting me as she flails. I hiss. I have slapped, put my hand over her mouth for a few seconds to try to make the sound stop. I confess that I often did not know what to do, how to respond. I confess that I have hurt her body by pulling an arm too roughly, holding her shoulders too tightly, wanting to shake her, stop her. I confess that I push her into the bathroom and tell her to take a bath so she can calm down. I confess that I go to my room and cry while she kicks the walls. I confess that I close the door and block it. I confess that I sit on the floor and cover my face. I confess that I tell her: "I don't know what to do."

But. It stops with me, must stop, will stop. Sometimes I sit with her until she stops crying. Sometimes I lock myself in the bathroom. Sometimes I threaten with punishments, to send videos to her teachers, shame her or call her a brat. I confess that I have lost my temper. I confess that I have behaved like a bad parent.

New ways of mothering. I invent what I never experienced. Trust that to stop it, I must innovate. And so, I have learned to sit and wait, to distract my child, to make her laugh, to say soothing things like "I know it's frustrating. I know you're sad. I know, I know." I sit and I wait. We wait for the beast of emotions to pass. This waiting, this soothing, this learning to bear the very piercing wail that activates my nervous system, that sends me swirling into memories of a hellscape. But this waiting, the switch reaching toward peace is not born simply from love. Like Lady Blood, who makes a field of corn, the origin of a people out of nothing, it is belief, it is magic, it is an indomitable core that says the world will not crush me—the underworld, Xibalba, will not destroy me, will not pass on to my children, use them to navigate. Although I may be born of it, Xibalba, is not my home.

Whatever mighty force I needed to stop the harm that happened to me, to my siblings, to my mother, to her mother, and whatever generation in whatever church or whatever missionary it happened to a child from an elder or from a priest or a nun, that force I found to stop it—I've found it.

Xibalba, The Maya Underworld

It stops here, my whole being says.

Whatever happened, I will spend a lifetime absorbing the violence into my body and finding ways to channel it back into the soil and deep into the earth, for it to turn into dust and be washed away by a thousand years of rain, heat, sediment, ice, smoke, and fire.

I give it back.

You, with the monstrous face, black eyes, long nails, body covered in steel or metal, stepping off a ship, dragging itself out of the water—you, conquistador, I erase you from the narrative. I blot your name out from the story.

You will not harm my mother, my grandmother, or her mothers. You will not harm my children.

You will not harm me.

Times I Did Not Speak

I experience times where I become my mother. I do not speak. I am mute.

It is 2011, and I am pregnant with my second child. The home-health nurse knocks on my door. She carries a briefcase, which I later learn contains the long needles, the medication, papers, and a tablet. What is your level of education? What is your ethnicity? Do you own this house? I answer her questions, prepare to remove my pants to expose my hip, to ready myself for the medicine I need so my body can keep the baby alive until she is ready to be born.

With my thigh exposed, and an embarrassing amount of my backside that has gotten accustomed to weeks of lying flat against a bed, the nurse, efficient like her practical blond bob, asks, Where do you store the used needles? Oh yes, I say. Let me get the container. It is hidden, high up in a cabinet, where my three-year-old daughter could never see it, where there is no chance she could touch it, be aware of it. It takes me a while to reach it, to pull it down, to bring it back to the nurse, patiently waiting with the needle raised in the air. She looks at me questioningly and I explain.

She looks at me carefully. We never let children play with needles, right?

I realize she is waiting for an answer. I realize that she thinks I might let my child play with needles, that she feels it is her duty and her honorable service as a nurse to Latina mothers to teach them about the danger of needles, children playing with them. I think of things I could say: *Did you read my demographics? Did you know that I am teaching a university class online from my bedroom while I'm on bedrest? I have a master's degree, bitch. Of course, I know that.* But she is holding the needle like she might not give it to me. I lie down.

Yes, I say, we should never let our children play with needles. I realize I am wearing a raggedy shirt, faded yoga pants. I remember that in the last year I have been mistaken for a maid or a nanny.

I remember the things that have been said to people I know who are or have been maids or nannies, or the things that were not said, like the friend's aunt who worked for a couple in River Oaks who never spoke to her but said Take It! while holding out their plates or glasses, and then letting it shatter to the floor if she didn't run quickly enough to grab them. Which she would then clean up.

She knew to not let children play with needles and she did not graduate high school, did not own a home, and lived paycheck-to-paycheck. Who am I to this lady? And if I am a stereotypical Latina, a Mexican American—or to the nurse, simply a Mexican or "Hispanic"—what is someone else who looks like me, someone else with darker skin, without the privilege of lighter skin? Who are we—Latinx people, Mexican Americans—to white people by just being ourselves?

What am I to anybody before I speak, or when I do? I am afraid I need to consider this. I am not sure I had considered this. Now is not the time to consider this because I want my baby to live and need the medicine which my doctor said will keep her alive.

I lie down on the couch. I remove my pants. I do not wince or move or cry out as she plunges the needle deep into my thigh muscle. Do not move for ten minutes after I leave, she says. She packs up. She comes back two more times, then ten more times, then every week until the baby is born: a total of 24 weeks, give or take for the times I'm in the hospital. I am so quiet when she handles me. I feel so quiet.

*

I'm too quiet in 1995 as well. In this linked present, my boyfriend, R. brought me stargazer lilies in crumpled green tissue paper. They were sitting in a vase where my mother had proudly displayed them in my bedroom, their sickeningly sweet smell and the thin layers of yellow pollen already dusting my bookcase. I was pretending to walk normally, careful steps that hid the pain, the bleeding.

I closed the bedroom door. I could not throw away the lilies. Everyone would know. He said they were my favorite, with my mouth full and when my mouth wasn't full.

They are your favorite! my mother cried when he brought them in.

He was dressed in pressed blue jeans and an emerald-green polo, topped off with a heavy whiff of men's cologne, the kind that cost the equivalent of several weeks of sacking groceries. Cool Water, maybe.

At fifteen, I still wore clothes from the children's department, size 13 or 14, depending on the brand we could afford. My shoes were tight the day he began with me, I remember—the day of the flowers, the days of flowers, the day of wearing too tight shoes, of the emerald green polo. They are not the same days but in my mind they are a single day of 1995, a series of images when I am fifteen and all the times, many and frequent and unwanted and nonconsensual, I remember as having spanned a year, a time period which may or may not be true. Many times compacted into a one-day memory, the course of a year. Those shoes—

shiny faux-leather Candies boots—were the best I had, besides my athletic shoes, the ones I wore for cheerleading practice and games. I loved those cheerleading shoes. I cleaned them with a washcloth, every smudge, all the mud and grass.

At fifteen, when had I been asked what my favorite flower was? I didn't remember being asked, or anyone even having considered what I liked. I don't' remember how it felt to wear the boots, only that they were tight. I don't remember if I threw them away. I don't remember when they stopped being my favorite shoes. I remember them as being identified as my favorite shoes but if I dissect this memory, they were my only other pair of shoes and I named them my favorite. I was supposed to have a boyfriend. I was supposed to call the life I was living my favorite because of the sacrifices my mother made to live the life I had of relative privilege and freedom as a girl.

Your shoes make your feet look like they are going to fall off your body, R. said later. Don't wear those.

I remember the first time I was raped as being the time I wore the boots, although it may not have been, but I remember it as being so. The manufactured memory is a fragment, a disparate shard when I see R.'s penis with horrific surprise. I am fifteen, and whether my mouth was full and I am on my knees or not, the shoes were my favorite, my only other pair. From memory, sometimes I could walk into school hiding the pain between my legs, my back, my throat, and, sometimes, when I couldn't, I fell asleep in Spanish class after lunch.

They were my favorite…. All of it was my favorite— the shoes, the flowers, the man—they said, in the narrative I construct out of a time of forming favorites, in the midst of being formed.

He brought the flowers every week for months. He raped me every day, and I was fifteen, and then I was 32, laying on the couch in the living room waiting for a shot of progesterone.

I kept a diary of every time he raped me, a little X with a number beside it, in case I got pregnant, in case I needed to decide when or how to kill myself. My diary becomes pages in my mind, that single day of 1995.

I tried to tell my mother. That single day, she was watching a telenovela and said before I spoke: If you open your legs, everything is your fault. You get what you deserve. She was talking to the television. She was talking to me.

Twenty years later, after my second daughter was born, my husband walked in with stargazer lilies. I set the baby down, screaming, milk dripping from my breast. I took the flowers and walked outside, threw them in the trash.

I have to tell you something later, I said. Why did you do

that? he said. I hate them, don't ever give them to me. I put the baby back on my breast. He is used to my strange rules that I can't explain. He sits next to me.

Over our seventeen-year marriage, more than twenty years together, I've been able to say some small phrases, as they fall out of my mouth fully formed, in bed, cooking dinner when the children can't hear.

It was that time when I couldn't look in the mirror—that whole year. Remember, I said? As if he had been there.

It doesn't make sense when it comes out, little bits of non-sequiturs, small, ripped notes left over, tucked away, in my mind. I stop. Some words should be unspeakable. Some words are not meant to have context, to make the listener comfortable; they are knife-filled, edged with violence, and smothering. Who wants to remember such things?

I don't even tell him the whole story. I don't even tell myself the whole story.

One night we are going to sleep, and he says, I wish I had known you then. I wish you could have told me. It is his way of saying he knows, not the story, but the way I had been broken and reshaped, and what I've had to do to keep myself alive. The belief I've kept aflame, sometimes barely, that my life was worth living, and that, because of this, I am his favorite kind of person. He is mine.

*

I have been patient with myself. I have been quiet and silent, the kind of person who is so soft-spoken at times throughout my life it was difficult for people to hear me, or too loud because I was unused to speaking in front of people and was awkward, nervous, too argumentative, too something not quite right in the right settings at the right times.

I cut myself off from the past so I could view it from some distant perspective where I was a new, different person. Yes, the past is gone—but despite how hard I tried, some things live on in the body, and I'd be walking in the grocery store, talking to my babbling toddler while feeling the avocados for softness, when my chest gets hot and heavy like I've been hit with a baseball bat because I see the back of her head across from me, standing there in front of the potatoes.

It could be D., my teenage best friend. My teenage lover. The girl in the story that led to the man, R., in the story—a puzzle piece leading to years of being raped, abused, then stalked, coerced, manipulated and undone. But it has never been her.

For years after I broke off our relationship, D. called my house, sent me hateful messages through fake accounts on Facebook. When this happens, suddenly I am not this capable woman, with an education, a list of accomplishments, a partner, a marriage, children, and a household we manage and love and nurture—but that girl who was made to feel like nothing, made to do things, believe things about myself, made to think some future I wanted was impossible for a person like me, things that can only be taught by another girl who finds and chooses those weak girls who will believe anything for a friend who makes them feel beautiful, for rapists they will call lovers.

*

It has taken me almost twenty years to wait for myself to say these words: I am a rape victim and survivor.

Like everyone else, I am complicated and am made of many things: I am the mother of three small children, a wife to my college sweetheart, with three siblings and a large Mexican American family; I have always rebelled against conformity in ways that felt comfortable to me, never worked well with authority figures but excelled academically in every way and am ambitious to the point where I make goals that others think are outlandish or unrealistic. I like doing things that people say I can't do, should not do.

I was a cheerleader (even though I was not and never was popular and didn't want to be) because I liked dancing and being around other girls and was not natural at making friends (and never had the money for ballet lessons or gymnastics). I married even though I'd promised myself I never would do so, but I met a gentle boy who was funny, had eyes the color of the shade of crushed bark, oak trees, who played guitar and ping pong, and wanted only what I wanted to give.

I had children under the same circumstances; I didn't want them and then I had them and was wrecked and tossed about by my love for them, a love that reshaped me into someone gentle, more open-minded. In so many ways, I thought I never would live this life, the one I have now.

As a young person, I prayed desperately for a life such as this, but wished for it in the way someone prays for an impossible dream, like a character in a V.C. Andrews novel, the kind I read obsessively as an adolescent, because I knew the understory: the darker one, where the girl never escapes, never frees herself from her awful circumstances, and lives her life out in some hell imagining different scenarios so she can survive.

I don't think anyone wants to say they are a victim, to acknowledge they survived something. To do so requires one to acknowledge and look at the fact that at one point you were overpowered, control had been exerted over you, and you were lost, severed from access to complete autonomy. I would argue: people fear this more than death (which is in of itself the ultimate loss of autonomy; however, it is easier to look away from death rather than the events in our lives that suggest one day we will die.)

Somehow our own annihilation seems more plausible.

Am I comparing rape to death? Maybe. Because when it happened, once and many more times, something in me died, again, and again. Not metaphorically. Each time I created a sort of new pocket, where I hid a dimension of myself, something that could not be destroyed, but also, more difficult to access. A maze within myself. I erased former versions of myself, saved fragments of the same version of myself despite my efforts to forget, and was left with what remained of myself.

Little pockets, rooms, corridors, constructed with compulsions that keep my anxiety at bay when I had triggers.

At 20 years old, a psychiatrist told me I would not live very long given a person with my history and the likelihood that another suicide attempt would eventually be successful.

I lived most of my 20s and 30s with bouts of deep

depression and psychosis, unable to keep a job—deeply private carrying a load of shame. Out of nowhere, I'd collapse into a trauma seizure. I couldn't be in crowds, and I struggled being around other people I did not know.

I cut myself. I drank with abandon. I put myself in precarious situations where I was drugged, and date raped. I forgot that I was a person. And when I felt more normal, productive, going about daily routines, I'd feel something emergently caught in my throat, sudden nausea, or panic, because I'd see a man like *him*, the same facial features, the same mustache and pocked face.

The smell of his lips, sweat, a texture from the touch of wood, grass, concrete, and there I was: my naked body in winter in the grass, under the light of an elementary school parking lot, on the hood of car, behind a factory or a dead-end street, clenching my teeth, blacking out and floating outside of my body. Until he was done.

I'd be 19 years old sitting in the middle of an English lecture; I'd be 32 years old holding my baby and wishing she had a different, healthier mother. I would do anything for these memories to go away, and for so many years, I did everything I could to make them stop, or at least, pretend that I didn't have them.

I did not want to be uncomfortable; I did not want to be pitied or looked down upon.

I did not want to be haunted. I felt profound shame for the incessant thoughts of self-harm, the deep belief that what had happened to me made me sub-human, less than an animal, a microparticle of an object.

So I let people believe, for twenty years, that once I was a girl who had a best friend from the age of 12 to 19 years old, and at 15, had a boyfriend, her cousin, who was five years my senior, and we did normal teenage things and had normal teenage experiences and I went to college and made a life like an average slightly middle-class and sometimes poor Mexican American girl. But this is not the case. This is the opposite of what happened.

Yes, I did go to college; yes, I became a productive citizen and not a criminal or an addict neither did I go down a tunnel of self-destruction that pulled down my family. But I am also other things, which includes the fact that once I met a girl in a middle school cafeteria, who turned to me and smiled, shared something with me, maybe a chip or a piece of candy.

I am learning how to look at the past—from this seemingly innocuous event, and everything after it that happened, up to the person I am today—and construct the story that will never be linear or straightforward but made of the mind's incredible power to warp and freeze time until we are able to heal: of what I did to live, from the time the raping began, and every single day afterward, when I made a choice each morning that I would allow myself to live another day.

To not cut as much, or as deep; to never again drive across town without stopping at red lights. To check myself into a mental hospital, to find a different therapist, a different psychiatrist, try another drug for depression and anxiety.

And most of all, to write, invent, create, find avenues into the mind where I could find my way out of my own suffering and back into the world.

Quinceañera

My mother made quinceañera dresses.

As a child, it was a common sight to see my mother hunched over a long bolt of white silk, taffeta, or tulle that bundled in her lap and onto the floor. While in the glow of the television which played *General Hospital* or a telenovela, she hand-sewed beads, trim, or some sort of accessory onto an elaborate dress.

This effort was done with intensity, despite her complete engrossment in the story she watched unfold on television, and all the while she shouted to the characters with warnings, imitated peculiar voices with uncanny accuracy, or let out a curse or death-wish to a villain who kept killing off her favorite characters.

*

I was named after one of those characters on *General Hospital* who died an untimely death, Dr. Lesley Webber, a character who finds a long-lost adopted daughter and dies in a car wreck in 1984 (only later to reemerge from a long catatonic state in 1996).

*

My mother never received any formal training in pattern making, or techniques, or how to sew and alter ball gowns, wedding dresses or quinceañera dresses. Yet she designed and sewed them all, hundreds—from the time she was a child and as a full-time housewife as an adult—except my own quinceañera dress, an event we could not afford after my family went bankrupt and lost our house and our car.

What she learned about sewing she did in an accumulation of years at her mother's side in the cramped sewing room at the back of their 1940's bungalow in North Houston, the Mexican area of town.

Her adopted mother, Guadalupe Ramos, lived on disability checks after her husband, Isabel, died. It was Isabel who wanted my mother as his daughter and chose her from the Catholic Charity hospital, but he died unexpectantly when my mother turned one, a few months after she'd been adopted.

Lita, as we called her, made extra income from sewing quinceañera and wedding gowns, and was known for her elaborate work, giant gowns full of tulle, a skirt hoop, lace, and all the show-stoppers—enormous puff sleeves, extravagant

Tiffany blue faux silk with lace and beads and ruffles flowing in cascading waves.

My mom learned to make her own clothes, and began helping her mother finish jobs to make income, in addition to learning how to speak English (Lita only spoke Spanish) and working odd jobs at the Catholic school she attended on scholarship. Lita's big plans for my mother included being ordained into the church as a nun, and becoming a full-time caregiver to her in old age.

My mother, however, fell in love with a musician, my father, and took what she learned to try to create a family out of very little cultural and social knowledge of how middle-income families lived, behaved, or raised their kids. In other words, she winged it.

She would make it up along the way, observing, mimicking, and teaching us how to fit in. Assimilate.

She learned how to become an accepted member of a more middle-class, multiracial community, when we were a young family and my parents were raising us in many ways foreign to the way they were raised.

We would find their ability to scrape and make-do useful later, when circumstances changed our financial stability, when my father lost his job and our family went bankrupt, lost everything we owned and lived off the charity of our extended family and friends; but when I was young, it seemed to me, as it does to most children, that my parents had it all together.

I did not understand until now that my parents, like most parents, were winging it; and part of what drove them to raise us or steer us into certain directions was their instinct to protect us combined with their ingenuity to make up what they didn't know how to do.

*

I learned early the importance of resourcefulness: if there is something you want to do, to learn how to do, or figure out, you spend time studying, observing, and gathering information and then try it.

If you don't have enough information, you try it anyway and aim to improve. I am certain I learned this from my parents, this earnest creativity that, underneath, was constructed from my ability to learn quickly and gain knowledge at a lightening quick pace.

My mother taught herself English by watching television, because in 1950s Houston there was no such thing as ESL or guided language learning in the schools she attended.

And my dad? He became a young father as he tried to complete his coursework, but the hurricane of responsibilities piled on top of him, and he was not able to finish his college degree.

Instead, he was an eager clerk in the mailroom of a corporate bank. Within a few years, he'd worked his way up through the bank and became a vice president by the time he was only 30 years old.

*

As a college student, I only had a nebulous idea of what becoming a writer would look like, and no desire to become a mother or wife.

I only had the desire to try without fail and for ten years this is what I did. I enrolled in a Ph.D. program in English, only to realize I did not have time to write, and so I dropped out.

I took jobs as a technical writer and journalist and eventually enrolled in a graduate creative writing program, but all the time I kept writing, studying, reading, and learning. I learned from my parent's and Lita's own tenacity to stay afloat, to build courage and bravery.

I was a graduate student at a prestigious MFA program when my husband and I decided to try to have a baby. It was a terrifying prospect, but less terrifying to me since I had been able to devote so much time to writing, and I felt that I could continue to cultivate this practice.

It would be an understatement to say that having my daughter undid me, shook me up, reshaped me.

I imagine most parents would say this; but I felt down to my core broken up and mixed all together.

*

For many reasons, I distrusted reading books about parenting. It seemed like a thing born of privilege, and an affront to millennia of mothers who raised children and families without textbooks and only each other. But where was my community?

It was only me, with visits from my mother and other family members in short periods, and hours and hours of being alone with my daughter while feeling overwhelmed with the responsibility of being her mother.

I was arrogant enough to believe I could figure it out; that when I held her tiny body against mine, some secret maternal mode would click into place. But instead, the first time I held her, saw her round face staring back beneath a wild fuzz of black hair, I felt unmoored.

The labor itself set off an immune response in my body that laid me in a long exhaustion, which would later be diagnosed as an autoimmune disease triggered by her traumatic birth, and on top of that, my mind fell into the cave of postpartum depression.

The desire to be a good mother was there, the desire to be tender and nurturing. I just didn't know how to do it, or how to set upon a new way of living that made sense to me. Those were years mixed with the dark cloud of grief—for the things I could not feel but wanted to—coupled with the joy of my daughter's sweet first years.

First Born

Her first week as a newborn, my daughter rocked contentedly in the electric baby swing, *Clair de Lune* playing in a robotic and staccato pace, part metronome, part disjointed lullaby.

I watched in awe. Her head was perfectly round, atop which flourished soft black hair like a cat's. Milk-fleshy cheeks, dark eyes and lashes, and a heart-shaped mouth that often paused in a round circle.

My baby, I repeated to myself.

When she held one eye closed, another open, she was ridiculously cute. Pirate baby, we called her. This five-pound girl, able to eat, cry, and digest but who could do little else, who fit in the crook of my forearm, who almost disappeared inside the chair of the padded swing.

She was everything I had wanted, down to the red birthmarks, the whorl of hair on her tiny back like the delicate pattern inside of a tree.

Oh, how terrified I was of her. There was so much I could do wrong.

This year, my firstborn child, M., is turning 13 and is a wildly creative, abundantly loving and fun person whose latest art project is Ka Pow, a set of trend-setting sunglasses for dogs that blocks the viewing of squirrels—illustrated with a blaze of color and flair, from the dog's wagging tongue to the wrap-around glasses which brilliantly protect the wearer's eyes from the unsettling image of their enemy, the squirrel, depicted as a disappointed, but darling, foe.

Recently as I sat next to M. in bed, looking at my child's latest sketches, M. said, Momma, out of all of the Mommas in the universe, the Mommas in parallel universes, all over, if I had the choice of Mommas, I would pick you, every time, as my own Momma.

I knew then (and cannot un-know now) that every single day that led up to being M.'s Momma was a day I was supposed to live. What world would this be without a M. in it?

Without all my children? And me, as their Momma, and also—just me, in this universe, in this version of reality, no need for alternatives. The kind of person who has been through what I have been through and can sit in the glory of a kid who can illustrate strange and hilarious ideas and dreams, the way their dad can play music, the way my dad can play music, the way my mother can sew a long-beaded train.

My own story, the real thing, with me, as I am, creating and writing and being my own flawed and dare I say, sometimes amazing, self. Can I say that? I'll say it. Damn it, I feel lucky to be alive, to have been a girl who wanted to die and tried to kill herself, but didn't, again and again, didn't.

NICU

The postpartum hospital room should have been numbered but I recall the door marker being blank, an empty placard without an identifying number or description. I could only find my way back from the NICU by following signs of the hospital wards, searching for the corner of a section of unused patient rooms, of which I'd been given use to sleep while my baby remained in NICU. I memorized the differences in the walls and floors in hallways as I went through this abandoned part of the hospital where I had been given a free room after the insurance covered the standard two-day stay after childbirth. The second night I spent alone, as my husband had gone home to be with our girls, and I decided to take the long way to the NICU from the new room. I'd had to sleep on a flimsy, foam sofa because the bed was broken and impossible for me to climb.

The hospital room had a broken bed and a small couch. The bed was stuck in its highest position, and the first night I was so exhausted from the C-section and feeding my baby every two hours, but I managed to climb the metal frame that held the mattress almost four feet in the air. I was barely able to walk at all, let alone climb the strange height of the bed, with the mattress reaching my chest.

That first night alone I clinched my fists and gathered all my strength to get through the pain that sought to make me faint or crumble into a ball. A splitting, a terrible burn, with the mouth of the flame sharpening into the wound, filling my abdomen with twisted spikes.

After thirty minutes, my hands clawing the sheets and biting a scream behind my lips, I climbed to the top of the mattress, where I collapsed and passed out from the pain, the blinding burn between my legs and at my incision site, like I had been torn open again. I set my alarm to wake in one hour.

Walking the series of long hospital hallways, mostly empty and in shades of white, grey-blue, cream earth tones, metal bars set against the walls to hold onto: each step I took toward my baby, being cared for in the NICU, sent waves of hot pain from the surgical cut through my body, making my consciousness swirl and look at what was before me as if through a window from the height of a skyscraper.

I whispered directions to that body as she walked. You want to see your baby. He needs you every two hours. He needs to feel your warmth, your love. He needs what milk you can give him.

I spoke to her as if through a straw, from the unnumbered room in a section of unused patient wing through every step on the walk, where the ends of hallways stretched and seemed to grow. She did not let her body clench, but while her incision sang and swelled, she held her fists into rocks, molten sediment, fingernails marking red lines into her skin. Every step to her baby. Every step to see her son and feed him, to make sure his breathing was improving. To hold him to her breast, skin to skin, and nurture his being with her body, however broken and imperfect she was as a person.

She could do this, I told her. She could bare this pain for her baby, this walk from one end of the hospital to the other. Usually there was no one in the hallway so if tears fell, she let them. As she neared the NICU section, she willed her face to relax. She wanted him to see only love and joy on her face.

How thrilling to finally reach the security booth at the entrance to the NICU, where she washed her hands, put on clean scrubs! He was near, and when she approached his nursery bed all of her leapt into her throat. So much singing when she peered into the bed and saw his tiny five-pound, ten-ounce body, covered in wispy black down, his fuzzy black hair covered in a cloth cap, and wires attached to his chest and his foot that pinged with the secret rhythms of his body. Carefully, she unhooked the wires to free him, then swaddled him against her bare chest behind a cloth screen.

I do not remember what she said in those quiet moments. His eyes, when open, were a gaze into rivers, lakes, a universe of stars. He drank and slept.

Cheerleading

It's when I'm flying, let go into the sky—my body lifted by multiple pairs of hands, then thrown up—that I find freedom. From this space, I can say who and what and how much. As a flyer for my high school cheerleading squad, my long dark hair flutters into angry Medusa tangles, my limbs jut up into the air like some kind of rag doll.

My mom watching in the stands with a mix of fear and pride. She is willing to allow the barely-there skirt, exposing my matching golden undershorts, because on my navel-gazing cheerleading top in capital black font I am labeled part of a team: Eagles.

I am part of a group of girls that dances and swings and tumbles along with a tidal wave of acceptable sexuality, though Mom calls it something else. I call it freedom, to assert myself to an audience as a sexual creature, with power over my body as to how and when I move it.

But I do not know that it is the beginning of a set of bars meant to trap me, then unravel me.

*

Floating reminds me of losing my body, getting lost in spirit and mind while the body hovers in some safe, untouchable state. A state of being that is familiar from the long summer days of childhood, squatting in the swamp weeds by the bayou with Y, us stuck together like June bugs.

My mud-smeared fingers, dirt curving into black half-moons under my nails, as I carefully inch up to my favorite inset. My friend would cry out from disgust. "Why you always messing with those nasty bugs?" But I knew she was as interested as me, only scared to touch them.

Y installed herself at my side as a helper. To pinch the perfect leaf-shaped grasshopper—brilliantly camouflaged in the bright green grass—before it leapt away. To carry the insect to my eager palm, sweaty and sticky from pulling up wildflowers, buttercups, the ones I'd carry home to mother.

And to feel the small weight of the insect dash from my loosening finger grip, and then with a squeal and hoot, grabbing Y's sticky hand, to chase its curve into the sky.

How we ran besides that muddy stream, scratching up our legs with wildflowers and grass, the sun pressing down its high summer rays like a thousand burning crowns. The thick air buzzing with mosquitos, the rattling of the cars and trucks as they passed the bridge on the other side of the bayou, passing our neighborhood for better ones, with trees, with fancy playgrounds, backyards with play sets and pools.

My skin would deepen to the color of clay, crushed cumin, more like my daddy's, and everything—the sky, the fences, the tidy front lawns and their proud perennials and monkey grass—my world tasted, smelled, glittered, seethed...of freedom.

My child's body, lanky and knobby-kneed, with bony arms, my back flanked by a tightly laced black braid—I wore tank tops and shorts and could move anyway I pleased under a sky that burned a bright hot 100 degrees—not with an indifferent glaze, but with blue-flamed promise that my body, myself, we, were part of the world as we were.

Oh, to be wanted in the world! I felt in those moments that I was loved and accepted, by the world, the universe, my small body on this spinning planet. It was a miracle to simply be next to my dearest friend, oblivious to the dangers that lay ahead of us in the years to come on the same streets and in the same houses, and that the gift of this childhood would provide a lifetime of loving memories.

*

Now, the drummers in the band pound out hard and ribboned jolts and rumbling growls that spike and quell the blood, shake the football field and the stands, and I'm alive when I hold onto the girls' shoulders and jump into their outlaid hands, after and when I stand up again and then when I am pushed up and released to the sky with their outstretched arms.

The band erupts into bass and horns, clarinets, a fury of sound spiking up my spine, entering my chest, all five feet of me, and without my thinking I'm being held up with two pairs of hands, my body in the air, one foot in one pair at a girl's chest, the other foot extended above the second girl's head. I raise my hands into a V, steady myself, knowing that the first girl is counting to four to extend my right foot above her head.

After the stunt, the girls count to drop me—one, two—and I fall, my whole body lowers on the plane of their hands as they squat together at the same speed and rate, and then with one quick movement, they throw my body up into the air. I land in their arms, which they form into a cradle for my descent. When I jump out of their arms to dismount, I twist my ankle but show no sign of the pain on my face. I jump up and down and yell chants to hide the bulging hot pain coursing in my ankle bone. The whole rest of the football game, I use that ankle until the pain is so terrible it makes me forget I have a body.

Pain is useful, I learn quickly. Breaking an ankle bone, spraining, shin splints, I run wearing weights on my ankles to build up my leg muscles and strength. I ignore my body's need for food, for water, for sleep. Because when I enter my house, the walls seem to close in, and I am my parents' daughter with a set of rules and expectations built on a religion I no longer believe in.

Running

The streetlights clicked on above as evening fell across our neighborhood, casting a running shadow onto the concrete as I pumped my legs as hard as I could go.

My chest hurt and I felt afraid of the upcoming streets, which had pockets of dark corners and apartments where anyone could show up from around a corner.

I kept running, even as the sky lost its glow and its purple tinge seemed to disappear as soon as I got going. I was a young woman running in the middle of the night, alone, with a ponytail that I had learned made it easier for attackers to grab a girl or woman with ease. I was without a weapon, in an area where women and girls were routinely assaulted, kidnapped, or worse.

I didn't care. I wanted freedom.

I ran until every part of my body ached and sang. My parents would be looking for me. They would be thinking I was out to meet a boy, which was their constant concern—my virginity, my risk of becoming sluttier. The way I dressed, the way I talked, the way I wanted to be wanted, my growing sexuality, all of it endangered me in my house, especially around my mother.

The limitations on who I could be and how I could behave as a girl, and how this set me up to be vulnerable and powerless, this reminder made me keep running. I felt lightheaded and aglow with my own power, ninety-five pounds and stupid, reckless, even, for running at such a time with who I was and where I was—but I had uncovered who I could be when I decided to run out of his car, from my parent's driveway, when the possibility of No suddenly seemed a reality, and that this was a gift that I had created from my own being—despite all that I had been trained to become.

Docile. Pretty. Attractive. Small. Compliant. Mature. I was still a girl. I wanted to be one again. I wanted to be the kind I had not thought of yet. So, I ran. I had become someone my mom didn't understand and couldn't be around, because she'd rather have the pretty girl on an older man's shoulder, a traditional Mexican guy who doted on her, all while raping her muñeca, a fifteen-year-old. I was no muñeca. No doll or someone's girl. I belonged to no one but myself.

The day after I was first raped, months before my nighttime run seeking a sense of freedom, the troop had training and we met on the track to run laps.

 I was quiet and said nothing to other girls as they slow jogged and sprinted while they gossiped.

Every single one of them had heard the rumors about me, and probably spread them too. When we readied for stunts, when I held onto their shoulders and jumped into the pair of two girls' hands, allowing them to lift my body into the air with their arms—I thought about landing with a kick to the chest or the eye, then remembered how a week before a spot had forgotten to check my back and I'd been saved an inch from breaking my neck.

I had strength, but I was always at some kind of mercy. If this was going to be my place, where I had found some sort of freedom, to be around girls where I could be myself in my body even to a small degree—I was willing to do it.

I was willing to give up this much. To be at risk of falling, to be at risk of being thrown without a safety net.

That year I sprained my ankle four times as I was thrown down from a stunt so quickly it twisted my foot. I'm sure it was broken at one point. I pretended that nothing was wrong, even ran with it that way, added weights so that my legs would become stronger, less aware of my own pain.

Eyes

Sometimes I wonder what would have happened if our eyes had not met in the rearview mirror, me in the backseat, you, a grown man staring at me with a steady gaze.

If I had not chosen that seat in the cafeteria. Gone to a different school.

If my father had not lost his job, and we didn't have to move.

If my mother stayed home at night those years, looked at me when I spoke. Found an interest in me.

If my bedroom door was kept open that day.

If the police officer stayed and asked me questions, instead of saying to him, Hey Cat, keep it cool, with a conspiratorial bang on the side of the door with his palm.

If one of our neighbors had called the cops or CPS.

If I had a different mother.

I carry the histories of my parents and grandparents in my present and past. My biological maternal grandmother was 15 years old when she was assaulted by a patient while working as a candy striper at a Houston hospital. Would she have been as vulnerable if her own mother had not died when she was a child, making it a necessity that my grandmother and her siblings work to survive?

The patient, my biological maternal grandfather, was in the hospital because his leg had been amputated after saving a girl from an oncoming train. His young cousin had fallen onto train tracks and he managed to save her by throwing her a few feet away into the grass, but fell himself on the same tracks, where the train crushed one of his legs. This accident sent him to the hospital where my grandmother worked, to the room which my grandmother would enter pushing a tray of snacks. What would have happened if he hadn't saved the girl, hadn't lost his leg?

I consider the fact that my paternal grandmother also lost her mother as a child, how she and her family faced racism in 1950s Houston despite being born in Houston and, much like my mother, attended schools that forbid Spanish from being spoken when that was her only language. She was terrified of my father and his seven siblings from experiencing the same trauma and refused to teach them Spanish, to do what she could to help them pass. My paternal grandfather also experienced language violence as a child, but also faced housing and job discrimination, even as a college graduate with a degree in engineering, belonging to some of the first Mexican Americans to attend the University of Houston. He served in World War II as a staff sergeant but came back to the United States only to face vehement racism that was acerbated by his darker skin in a fiercely segregated city. How has my inheritance of these losses, of these violences, affected my susceptibility to being vulnerable, to being a descendant of violence so momentous it is carried in my body?

If my biological grandmother, age 15, was left alone the day she worked at the hospital. If her mother never died.

If my biological grandfather had not saved a girl from an oncoming train, then fallen on the same tracks to lose a leg—sending him to the hospital where he met my grandmother, a candy striper bringing in a tray of snacks.

*

It is possible that there are different versions of me living vastly different lives from this one in various universes.

In every single version, I'd like to think there is some existential core to myself, the one that loves her father unceasingly, the one that laughs and sings and dances with those close to her, the one who does not refer to herself in the third person, the one who writes, the one who loves four people as an adult which made the past melt away to mud.

I hope this life is the only one where I had to invent mothers for myself, where No did not exist when it came to my body, where I had to find No, where I had to mother myself by becoming a mother.

Out there, among the stars and unseen planets, there are thousands of me as a teenage girl thriving, playing instruments, singing and hiking, reading, finding friends and loves, experiencing heartbreak and sunsets, years rolled out in one joyful stream, and never once being beaten, pinned to the floor, a life for which I believed there was no exit.

*

But didn't I choose the seat? Meet the eyes? I was the one who learned to hit back, to hurt the way I was hurt in return. I must have had choices that I didn't take. I ended up where they said I would. Who was I to ask for something else? But I escaped—my mother, my abusers, my entrapment.

I am still escaping.

A Poem

Drumbeat (One)

standing tall at the chalked sideline, she's the smell of grass cut down, the whoosh of boys mowing down other boys. at the tip of it, full grass skirt, grass creeping up the limbs, more grass poking out like straw, i stand above the crowd. mom says this is it, baby. how do they want it? it's the surrogate who is flung into sky, her legs pointed to the horizon, one foot east, the other west. both encased in white converse sport numbers, thumb-licked clean. & inside her flung belly the daughter of her mother, both herself and the mother her daughter. the stadium points and shouts, the mother points and points. the daughter and the daughter she carries. those! those! mine! and what's that sound we hear? the crowd roars.

Drumbeat (Two)

the bass a thunder to the hips, so near to cracking. watch this, move aside, and the daughter (the one under the skirt and the one smiling for it) can move like no one's business, like they say, she will break it all the way down for two hours straight. drum punches, full drum line, horns and all the way back up. you have not seen such a scrawny thing work the bass and percussion nor hips nor stick legs to name the beat. but the muscles are birthed from ankle weights, at night, with splits against baseboards. let them crack me, let her, the body said. i'm good for it, the cymbal toss to soften and full stop. she flings herself. it can't last, it won't finish until she breaks. yet she flings and flings her only good thing, this body. then, she knew, always did, that it belonged to her mother, to others. and for an escape she'll be shredded, flag girl that beats & beats past torn shreds. the last beat that sets her to flee. the last beat that begs to stay.

Medusa and Lady Blood

Our minds are malleable, creators and artists—if our bodies are frantic, seeking safety, an end to a nightmare, our minds will wander, run, search for rest that our bodies will not give us. We use all our tools at our disposal to survive. I'm thinking of Medusa, Malinche, or La Llorona, monstrous women of legends described as murderers, ghastly in personage or horrifying in their actions that defy all that is good and holy. A woman made so monstrous in appearance that her looks turn men to stone. A woman who drowns her own children, forced to roam imaginations, rivers, the railroad tracks, moaning in despair for a world that makes desperate mothers more desperate.

Before they existed as symbols, they were, and still are, everyday women—praying in a temple, shopping at a market with a baby strapped to their chest with a scarf, breastfeeding a newborn in a sleepy haze. Then their lives are beset with nightmare. Medusa is violently raped in the temple of Athena and is punished by being made into a monster, made to live a life of darkness and silent rage inside a cave. Malinche marries her

rapist and births a nation out of despair and survival, even begins
to love the people who enslave her; her life is haunted by guilt,
the desire to love, the desire to find happiness within the cage
of her life. La Llorona searches for the sacred connection torn
from her by circumstance and abuse, wailing from the profanity
of mental illness and the choice she made to save her children
from lives of hell without a father's name and protection, in a
culture where without these they were bound to poverty and
shame.

*

These mythical women look like monsters, are the epitome
of a psychopathic or unholy mother or woman, but the mirror
that reflects them makes demons out of women because they
speak, move, challenge then decide to act, however desperate,
despite the chains around their necks. In their own mirrors:
women who want to pray in safety, in peace, and the violent
theft of that right in body and spirit; women who are enslaved
and make a life worth living with their bodies, sectioning off
their minds into intricate tunnels of survival skills; women who
experience traumatic childbirth, lost in the haze of postpartum
depression, when all the people they love disappear and the
floor drops away from her feet.

These women are hungry for the sacred, for the rooms torn
from them from which they pray. They are made to be profane,

but this profanity is shaped against their search for the sacred even amidst the nightmares that, to this day, threaten to destroy their very being.

I have been called monstrous. In my own mythology, I am like Medusa, Lady Blood, La Llorana, as I morph their stories and the stories of my ancestors with my own. I will search and wander. I will shape my body against a rock. I will mourn the children who died when I was sick in the mind and spirit. I will search for my ancestors in the faces of the children I bear with a rapist, a colonizer, with a people who've committed mass genocide—I search for something worthy of life.

What is monstrous is behind the mirror, the people holding it up, the mirror itself tainted with blood and violence.

Dear D.

I was a child when we tried out friendship,
me, curling your hair, you lining my eyes
with eyeliner that you burned with a match

making it soft and dark on my eyelids.

You were breathtakingly beautiful, with an abundant black swoop
of hair, hearts for eyes, and men and women stopped to look at you

in the streets, driving, mouths open, watching your hips,

the pleasing curve of your mouth. They asked to touch your hair,
hold your hand, cradle your breasts. You loved the attention, even as a child.

But you did not want that, though you let them.
You wanted me, a girl that looked like a child
for far longer past childhood.

Skinny and pale, you told me to stay ugly.
I believed that as true, your ugly for me.

It wasn't my appearance: the long wispy, dark brown hair, my wide eyes,
generous and believing, I was not unpleasant to look at.

Once, when we were 13, I was on the stage
for a show for the drill team, a show you did not make
because you were not a good dancer.

I knew how to commit my body to leaps, to throw
myself to the ground as if floating. I danced like my bones were on fire.

I found you in the audience where you shamed me:
my childish body, my bones sticking out like a skeleton.

You turned your own lack into my own.

I hated you for it, but became more loyal and protective,
as the girls and boys at school started to hate you
for stealing their lovers. The boys hated you for being a dick tease,

for fucking, for not fucking, for being fuckable.

I was 15 when your mother told me to get you
off your father's dead body that lay in the hospice bed
so he could be taken to the morgue.

Your mother said I was the only one who could do it, tear you away.
You did not forgive me for tearing you away from him.

Dear D.

Your father treated you like a queen, his doll, and your mother was always jealous. She wanted you dead as much as you wanted yourself dead. I heard after his death that you would go out into the street at night and stand in the middle of the road, wanting to be hit by a car.

I decided I did too, because even in your grief, your grip grew tighter, more suffocating, cruel

and burrowed, a deeper knife.

*

I told the girls who wanted to jump you where you would be that day. Every day at lunch you spent most of the hour spraying your hair, applying make-up. Staring in the mirror.

They found you. Pulled your hair over your face and gave you a black eye, scratched your face, smothered you with your own hair.

*

You knew it was me who told them where you'd be. I knew it was me. I was monstrous.

And that is when I began doing whatever you asked, however you asked.

I dated your older cousin, who raped me in the winter on an elementary school parking lot.

I let you fuck me with pillows on my head and I was disgusted and turned on, a combination that both shamed and shocked me.

You smelled like meat, or honeydew, or forest. Your cousin smelled only of meat, of oily mustache. I loved you.

*

He showed us porn in his bedroom with his door locked and his parents in the house.

I had just learned what a penis could do. I had looked it up in the dictionary.

I thought this was sex.

I thought we were in love. You and me, Him and me. He raped me repeatedly. When I broke up with him, you asked me to come over to give me a card with two hundred dollars asking me to come back to him. I ripped it, then realized he was behind me. I hid in a closet until he left.

*

At 18, you were angry with me. You found out that I was going to Rice University and said I couldn't go.

You kept calling me to save you from your mother. I would drive across town to find your mother throwing your clothes onto the lawn again and sit with you while your entire family came over to hear your mother call you a whore.

*

After your father died, I took care of you. I would stay at your house or be called over by your mom or brother. I would sit with you, I'd rock you, I'd try to bring you back.

Your mother had a strong dislike for you, a perverse jealousy for the way your father adored you, and with his death, she let any semblance or gesture of motherly affection fall away.

Come get her, she'd say on the phone to me. I have no problem putting her on the street if she doesn't snap out it.

*

You were allowed to stay at your mother's house. You stayed and I left.

It took me a year for you to stop stalking me, after I stopped talking to you. I wanted to go to Rice. I wanted to live a different kind of life.

I did everything I could to avoid you, but you started showing up behind my car early in the morning as I got ready to drive to work. I closed off. I drove away. I didn't answer your calls. I blocked your number, blocked the new numbers you called from. Threw away your letters without opening them.

You became a sex worker. I remember you could not read very well. If I had stayed longer that day, if I had said Okay, I won't go. Would I be with you still? Would we be running the streets? Would I be trying to forget like you? I heard you were in jail for theft. I heard you were in jail for soliciting. I did not take the money, even though I needed it.

You found me on Facebook and sent me a message about my daughter, whose picture you saw. I wanted to crush my computer, to set it on fire. I am always afraid you will show up on my doorstep. My nightmares are then ones where I let you walk in.

D.

I wanted to believe what she said. I also, equally, was terrified that if it didn't come true, that she would make it true or she would kill me. She said we would always be together, into our old age, her pet lesbo, and we would take care of each other like no one else could.

I once called her from a gas station pay phone after I'd attempted to run away from home. I could see my dad circling the street corner to find me and I hid on the floor of the convenience store, then in the bushes on the side of the road. She came immediately. She always came immediately, in my mind. But in reality, that had been the only time, and I was the one who came immediately. Even if I had to drop everything and drive an hour to get to her. She needed me. How could I let her be entrapped by the violence she was constantly surrounded by?

*

When I told her what happened that winter at the elementary school parking lot, she said it was my fault. That every time, it was my fault.

For getting in his car. For continuing to get in his car. I was tired of seeing my father drink himself into oblivion for the fact I was no longer a baby. I was tired of not having a mother available for even the smallest gesture of care. I kept going and kept going. I could not walk some days at school. I felt spilt open with the things he'd put into me, the sheer force. I walked to the counselor's office every day, for a month, sometimes two or three times a day. She was never in her office.

*

There were teachers, friends, adults never available to me. I became disrespectful in class or slept on my desk. I didn't read or do homework, not until it got close to the end of my relationship with R. Something woke up in me. I'd written something in English class and a teacher said I was talented, that I could become an author, that she believed I would. I was slowly being exposed to writing by women of color, Amy Tan, Maya Angelou. I decided that I would close all the doors to the place I found myself in and get out through a window.

*

D, we were reckless with each other. I did love you, and I also believed love meant letting someone behave recklessly with me in every way. Until I decided to stop it.

Marcus

You're not leaving me, he said. I'd opened the screen door and stood on D's front porch, she and her brother standing behind me snickering.

Go away, I said. Did you walk here all the way from your parent's house? You're crazy.

His clothes were soaked in sweat, and his face seemed set on a move. He must have walked for two hours to reach D's house, more than the length of the entire city and then some.

The door creaked as I moved to step back. Then his hand was around my wrist. You're not leaving me. I was on the small front lawn then, face in the grass, being held from the back by my arms. He was short, a few inches over five feet, but he was muscular with thick arms and legs. A gymnast, as easy as breathing, he could do a back flip with one hand or punch a hole through a wall.

D and her brother had stopped laughing.

Red Lights

My grandfather stared as he sat in front of a sandwich on a plate, a glass of water paired with it, which my mom had set before him on our kitchen table.

He seemed lost, not just by time and sense, but by this forest of a life that he saw no longer contained World War II, fried chicken, bars, his sons and daughters coming in and out, their guitar playing, his wife's pouf of black hair and doe eyes, the back of her as she prepared dinner.

Instead, a table, at which he sat at alone, an unknown woman serving him in what looked like a sterile place, maybe a factory, and no idea where one is to relieve oneself in this kind of place.

*

I had just returned from the mental hospital. I carried inside myself a rock of safety and offered it to him. He said the war is over, while my brother, still a preschooler, ran his bike in circles around my grandfather where he sat outside on a lawn chair.

He took that stone and threw it, using his good arm, pulling it way back and over, the strong powerful man whose deep laughs were full of leather, beer, and wild love. No one has ever been able to hold me the way he once did.

Before he died, I prayed to his spirit: Grandfather, you don't have to visit me when you are dead. I had set you inside the stone, the one you threw and which I saved. I am not ready to lose anything, even if it is painful, heavy, and best be left lost. I keep you and this stone, together. I swallowed the stone whole and it has calcified, a living organ, that beats like a violent sea. I keep you safe inside me.

*

1998. On the day of graduation, I was sitting in my high school commencement ceremony praying for my period. Dear God, I said, in a childish voice to no one, hoping for pity from the universe. Only this and I promise.

I walked across the stage, more than 10 medals jingling against each other on my small chest.

I imagined that the man who had raped me just three years earlier was in the audience clapping for me, along with my boyfriend, my family, my grandpa in a wheelchair, all proud of me, and I was right.

Later that man sent me a letter praising my achievements, a stack of twenties tucked inside, something he had tried before to win me back. When I sat back down in my chair among the 700-plus graduating class, I felt a surge of merciful warm fluid seep through my thin gown. My boyfriend, who had just faked an injury to escape military training, would dump me a week later.

*

I'd like to understand everything that led me, at 19, to find myself laying in a bed across the room from a stranger, a woman at least twice my age, retching, delirious, smelling of vomit and piss, as she detoxed from an alcoholic binge.

*

Because I drove to my parent's house in a daze without stopping at any red lights or stop signs. I was 19 and had never said the word rape in my mind, associated it with myself in any way, and it would take me almost fifteen years to realize from the time when I made this forty-minute ride to my parents from across the city, a time when and the numbers were adding up to something I couldn't calculate.

My parents were sleeping. I am a committed person. My mom taught me to always keep my word. I had committed to ending my life, but decided my parents needed a chance to stop me. It wouldn't be an attempt. I was too strong to do anything half-assed. I would do it, and that would be it. The pain, that sharp cut through the half of me, was getting too searing to walk around with day to day and there was no way I could touch it, see it, move it; I just knew it was there and I wanted to be free of it.

*

My parents woke up with me standing over their bed, the same bed frame that they had had since I was a little girl, a brown ornate faux wood headboard with curls that I used to trace with my fingers when I crawled beside my mother the times I couldn't fall asleep. My father tried to talk to me, Tell me what's wrong. Take me, I said, or I'm not going to be here anymore. I remembered that girl that once was my parent's daughter and I was no longer her. I had stopped being my parent's daughter in 1995.

*

Freshmen year, my English teacher hated me and said something insulting to me that day, so for the rest of class I acted up, made jokes about her with my classmate and drew cartoons worthy of a Jerry Springer script, making fun of all the teachers. (This comic, though hilarious, got me suspended.)

I put a wad of gum in the long black hair of the girl sitting in front of me, forcing her mother that night to cut it shorter.

I asked to go to the restroom toward the end of class and

didn't come back.

*

I walked to the counselor's office and stood trying to understand that sign that said she was not there. I went back to her office later that day and the same sign on her closed door was still there. I went back the next day, and the next, and by the end of the week, I realized I was never going to be able to say the thing, and I didn't even know what thing it was I needed to say or how I could say it.

Even the thought of saying it made me want to go run into the middle of Antoine and let a car run over me. I went back to class and stopped looking for anything to stop. The effort to stop it was like asking me, a 95-pound teenager, to bench-press for the Olympics or box a grown man. I floated away, became without-body.

*

I know how you got those skid marks on your legs, my English teacher said. You Mexicans like to have your babies young.

*

My parents called me a whore when I lied to them about where I'd been, when I came home wearing skimpy clothes smelling of sweat and lies. What have you been doing? my mom said. Remember what happens when girls open their legs. They get what they deserve and I'm not helping you one bit.

*

My grandmother's purse hung heavily on the doorknob, and I'd run and drag it back to her. I have a purse like it, a white leather one, which I hang on our doorknob to the annoyance of my husband, who likes to close the laundry room door shut and has to move my heavy purse out of the way to do so. I hang it back there after he moves it. At my grandmother's house, I would reach my hand inside her purse and find some object, some treat that she'd picked up at Woolworths for me, which had waited in her cushiony purse until I came to see her. I would sit in her lap, her giant eyes watching me from beneath a pouf of dyed soft black hair, hair she let me, my sister, and cousin brush and set into sponge curlers.

*

When someone touches my hair with reverence, the kind only a child has for someone she is preening, I am filled with such a flush of tenderness that my body, so often ignored, is suddenly present. There are moments when my body wakes up, when it sits up and sniffs the air and salivates.

One moment is now: as I sit here writing, thinking in one hour I must leave to pick up my children from their school day, and that our days will continue in a series of snacks, meals, restroom breaks, baths, soccer, ballet, running outside, swings, playgrounds dances, movies, pushing them around in laundry baskets like a train, play dates, arguments, crying, burning dinner, and singing. M will draw and draw, L will sing and litter the floor with toys and acorns, leaves, and tape collages of hearts and demons and rainbows to every chair. C will wheel everything from room to room, make everything go until he falls from tiredness.

*

This morning, like many others, I wake up with a body run by that old train. I am slow and move through deep pain, an ancient pain, urgent enough that I can't use my regular acting skills. I am a total bitch to everyone, everywhere, and I don't care, because my chest hurts as if I'm being crushed, and it makes me lose my breath. I help get our children ready for school while my husband looks at me warily.

*

Most people would immediately go to the emergency room if they felt the common pains I have had, and before I knew what my body was doing, I often did, where the ER physicians did nothing but patronize me. Now, it is daily living with a body, for whatever errant code sending messages to inflame and attack myself, to make me limp or strain to use my hands or feet, to see—this is the make-up of the regular me.

I am used to ignoring my body—from the simple cues of hunger, the need for sleep, the urge to relieve myself, to the larger cues of severe pain, cutting discomfort. As a mother and woman, this is rewarded and even used as a badge of honor.

I'd learned the important skill of floating away from the body, often used by soldiers or survivors of war and trauma: living, day by day, by pushing past physical and emotional pain, that, if acknowledged, will cost you your life.

*

But this skill—bodily invisibility—kept me alive for many years. If I could keep my body moving, not acknowledge the way my body felt and wanted from day to day, I would live. If I acknowledged it, I would show awareness of what was happening to me, what had happened to me, and I will fall into a whirlpool of self-destruction.

*

For thirty-eight years, I not only lived doing this, in the eyes of our culture, I thrived. As a younger person, I became an extremely good student because of it—ignoring sleep, ignoring hunger, dedicating all my time to studying, dance, and friendships—and was very thin, which was also rewarded.

I graduated in the top 1% of my graduating class out of more than 700 students (albeit from a high school of mainly students of color and was not seen as the emblem of quality education in my city).

For years, I barely slept, ate one time a day, pushed my body to its physical limits in dance and cheerleading. And this skill continued to be rewarded in college. Coupled with barely eating or sleeping, it allowed me to earn a 4.0 grade point average while working multiple jobs, and taking 15 hours of classes. I was rewarded by being able to transfer to an elite university, where this behavior was commonplace among students.

*

As a woman living with an often-debilitating autoimmune disease, an inflammatory condition that can affect my vision, walking, muscles, and energy, I must be keenly aware of simple cues of hunger, tiredness, and body aches, so that I can take care of my body and keep from getting worse. This is a new practice for me. I am used to only the constant push, to go along with the motto emblazoned at the gym to Work Harder Work Stronger.

I learn to become present, aware, and uncomfortable in this wilderness of a body, and calling it myself.

I know only it is a good day if I can lay with a wrecked body and move my antenna around in bed next to my husband, look at him out of the corner of my eye while he's reading and realize that this—all this—has no repeat button, no rewind or replay, no matter how many videos or iPhone pictures he takes, no amount of Facebook posts, or selfies with kids, none to change that we don't get it again, and the feeling of that settles into the greatest pain of all—that ancient pain, the one gifted to me from my mother, grandma, my sister and all my aunts—and I sit with it, curl up to it, try not to let it crawl between my husband and me as we cradle to sleep, or get near my daughter when she slides into bed during the night saying in my ear—I'm so scared, Mommy. I am so scared—her lantern in hand that she clutches while she sleeps, tossing, and that long shadow it casts on the floor—It's nothing, nothing to be afraid of, I say, and we kiss and we nuzzle and all night long I dream different versions of, Don't let it stop, don't let this loveliness end please.

We started this, I laughed once. We made them. We make this.

Face in the Window

For the three months I lay in a hospital bed, I was surrounded by hands.

I was at the Women's Hospital of Texas for a pregnancy that involved preterm contractions and a baby's faltering heartbeat. There was my hand under my head, growing numb and uncomfortable, while I lay on my left side for weeks to protect the blood flow to Lily.

There were hands of nurses, plunging needles of hormones into my arms, pricking my fingers for blood to test my blood sugar level, moving my legs and arms, strapping my pregnant stomach with belts and monitors. Doctors' hands, searching for the baby's heartbeat with a stethoscope. Hands quickly and with efficiency examining the tenderness of my cervix to determine my readiness to deliver. Hands infecting me with viruses, infections with their constant examinations.

*

Everything was done with care, but without the care of human connection. It couldn't be. Hospitals are made for passing through, to monitor and mend the body, not to care for a patient's well-being.

*

At night, I watched the window that faced another hospital building, blocking most of the sky and, always, the moon. It saddened me to lose sight of the moon for so many months. Those nights, I saw a person pay constant vigil to another patient, the person's silhouette in the window of the other building across from my own. I counted on seeing this shadow every night, as I repeatedly pressed my cell phone to see my daughter's two-year-old face light up the screen. If I couldn't sleep, I would play a three-second video of her, an oval face glowing in the dark hospital room, her eyes deep buckets of night. Hi Momma, Hi Momma, Hi Momma.

*

The pain was so powerful and seemed so endless that I thought for sure I would die. And the loneliness, especially being away from my husband and my two-year-old daughter, made me feel as much pain, mentally and emotionally, as I did in my body.

As difficult as it was to be away from my daughter, I couldn't hide my pain from her, or anyone, and I was grateful she couldn't see me often in the hospital. The pain was constant. I had spent several months at home on bed rest, until I felt searing pain in my pelvic bones, contractions that never went away, that came back to tighten my abdomen in its angry squeeze. The pain of the baby's foot lodged into my cervix almost made me pass out if I tried to walk.

The nurses helped me to the restroom or held up ice or a cup of water to my mouth. Once when the nurses did not appear fast enough, there I was like an animal, crawling on the floor to the restroom, interrupted because of sudden unexpected pain in my cervix. When the nurse found me weeping on the floor, the doctor prescribed medicine to sedate me and numb the pain.

Thankfully, I didn't experience this level of pain again until I went into labor. But often, I had to fend for myself for simple tasks, such as drinking sideways from a straw. The water would dribble down my chest or into my face.

*

Many of the night nurses would come in at 3 or 4 a.m., when I would obviously be sleeping, and turn all the lights on in my room, bursting in without a greeting to jam medicines into my mouth or adjust my monitors. There I would be, my hair usually tangled and sticking to one side, heavily pregnant and groggy, jolted awake and frightened every time. I felt reduced, below the level of a human. Take this, they'd say. And in silence they left, turning off the lights as quickly as they'd left them, or sometimes, forgetting altogether to turn them off.

*

I watched hours of reality television—toddlers at beauty pageants, families living in trailer homes with Southern accents being made into a spectacle, the lives of little people—and felt even more poor from it. Everything was on stage, people being exploited or used. It was better than the news, stories of women and children found murdered or abused, a constant barrage of stories of violence against the vulnerable.

I watched the monitors as the contractions approached, watched the baby's heart rate fall dangerously once again. All previous prayers I had ever said felt like non-prayers compared to this. But there was no divine presence in my room, especially at night, just the glow of the television, bright hall lights from under the door. Every day the woman who cleaned my room said, God bless you, before she left the room. It felt like an insult, though I know she didn't mean it as one.

*

My prayers were simple: Let me out. Let the pain stop. I will be a better mother, I swear.

Though I am a converted, practicing Jew, I grew up Catholic, the punishing-you-are-going-to-hell kind. I had sinned. After my first daughter, for more than year I had been low with postpartum depression. I held her like a duty, kissed her in the middle of the night when no one was watching to ensure that she knew, somewhere inside, I was a good person and could love her. I was laying punishment onto punishment. I did not know what a mother should be, and intrusive thoughts harangued me as if from a demon: *You are an awful person. You're the lowest creature on the planet.* I got better, but somehow the remnants of that time came back to find me during my second pregnancy. Now it manifested as pain.

*

Now, the pain felt angry because I was too. Angry that I still did not know what it was to be a mother, that I felt orphaned, that the pain felt like punishment because of my own poverty of human connection.

One day, my mother visited. I have such a migraine, she said, looking at the television and suddenly laughing at a commercial. Oh, that reminds me of something….

She told a story while I lay, as if it were a choice, frozen in pain. A beep from the monitor chimed and a nurse came in to check the contraction strips. They were still three minutes apart. The nurse gave me another shot of Brethine, an asthma medication that helped slow and ease contractions but made my teeth chatter and my body shake as if I was naked in a tundra, my body shaking against the metal rails and creating a shudder of metal clinks. As my mother continued talking, I shook her out.

*

That night I prayed hard to the person in the window, the one who sat in vigil, who'd become my symbol of divinity. My stomach squeezed and burned. And as I prayed, something happened. The person turned to face me, the dark of their face fuller than any light that had poured in the room before. I knew my room was completely dark, and most likely they could not see me at all. But the possibility was there, that sometimes they could see me, and wanted me to know that they saw me, and in return, I could look back. They saw me and was not turned away by the frightening figure that I made. That was enough for me.

I felt forgiven, and forgiving, for that simple look toward me. An acknowledgment, a recognition.

*

I knew it was a stranger, that this was something less than the real connections I had with my own family. But, in my mind, it was a divine sign to me that I would survive. My mind turned in that moment to believe that I could and would.

Some people need divine presence in their life, an angel of God to visit their bedside in a Technicolor glow. I didn't want or need that. I just wanted something human—sight, touch, speech—something that I could give back.

In the hospital, it had felt like that basic human connection had been taken from me as I was pulled and prodded. But the person in the window was a signal from the universe that I was seen, that I could be seen as I was.

The contractions finally became less risky to my baby's health, and I was released to go home three months from the time I was admitted. When my husband came to pick me up with my daughter, to take me home to finish bed rest there, I was ready. I was prepared to accept whatever additional pain I would face through the last weeks of my pregnancy, and I was prepared to accept the fear. The face in the window showed me the presence of the divine. It existed in the people around me, every day—my husband and child, those who waited for me to grow and trusted that I would.

La Llorona

My mother stopped the car on a bridge overlooking Greens Bayou. Get out, she said. She threw a backpack of my clothes in my lap and reached over me and shoved open the car door. I fell out like a duffel bag. She drove off with the door half open, swerving as she sped away. I stood there with one strap hanging onto my shoulder, hoping my worn copy of *Flowers in the Attic* was still stuffed at the bottom where I'd left it from the morning.

*

I loved that backpack—hot turquoise, my favorite color, covered in black sharpie drawings of swirls and figures and my name in block letters. "How could you do this?" my mom said. "You have no respect for the money we spend on you, the food we spend on you." My mom woke me up for my first day of middle school, holding the brand-new backpack covered in illustrations. I liked it even more, and I felt elated to leave the house after the summer months of being stuck at home alone.

My mom screaming as I walked out of the house to go, the bus stop turned to noise.

*

When my sister and I shared a bedroom, in the house that we had once owned, my mom let us paint one side bubble-gum pink—my sister's favorite color—and my side an equally bright turquoise. For a while, a few months, our room looked like an art installation where one side my sister monopolized the phone and the closet and on the other, I tried to prevent her from using the Nintendo and the bedroom door. (I failed.)

When she turned fifteen, she'd put a piece of tape down the center of the bedroom to indicate which side was hers and which was mine. I let books, dirty clothes and socks, shoes, papers, wrappers and stuffed animals accumulate on the tape to prove a point, and give her crying fits. Who wanted the world as she saw it, tidy and organized by color?

It was the year of her quinceañera. The one I wouldn't get later.

*

Our lives were not a sitcom. My parents let us see *Child's Play* and *The Shining*. No movie was off limits from the time we were born. We were shocked by nothing, and even Mom's violent rampages were as normal as drinking a Dr. Pepper for breakfast. My parents got married when they were both barely adults, really still teenagers. My dad was a musician, but he gave up his talent for a desk job at a bank, and did well enough to become an executive at a young age where drinking beyond control was like wearing a business suit.

*

I used to shine his shoes to a bright sheen, could see my face in its mirror. The best moments of my childhood are with him in it, hearing him play "Daddy's Home," Chicano blues and 60s rock on the guitar, or reading a book with him at bedtime. But he disappeared behind beer and liquor, his own sadness, a pathological tendency for depression that I inherited.

My dad's love has sustained me. I think he thought he could save my mother, thought he had, from the hell that she'd come from. He didn't see or denied that she brought hell with her.

*

If my mom could, she'd write a story with a completely different version of reality. She says I lie, that all my memories are false.

She never left us at home by ourselves.

I never let myself in with a key and stayed by myself for

hours every day after school.

She never chased us around the house with a leather belt, grabbing us by the hair, the ankle, the arm, to beat us for spilling milk, talking back, arguing with each other, or talking while she watched a soap opera, or not listening, or listening when we shouldn't, or refusing to go to the bathroom for too long, or for being in the bathroom too long, or being too loud, for crying, for laughing, for standing, for Stop that right now or you'll see how mean I can get, for dirtying up clothes, for her having to wash our clothes, make our food, Don't you know I wanted to do something else with my life, and the worst was when the beating was followed by a longer punishment, liked being locked out of the house and in the backyard, summer mid-day in Houston's 100 degree heat, no water, no food, the door clicking when Dad got home.

She never punched us in the head, the stomach, our bodies, never made us cry until we were hoarse and went silent from pain.

She would never jump out of a moving car and throw her wedding ring down a ditch at night, and definitely not multiple times while we waited on the side of some busy road. She never left us in the car at midnight in the middle of downtown to drag my dad out of a bar. She never locked him in the garage. There were lots of things my mother says she never did.

There is nothing to forgive me for, she said to me once. I've done nothing that needs forgiveness.

*

I flinch when someone touches the back of my head and I'm not expecting it. My heart stops and chills hearing a glass shatter, liquid spill. My body says something different than what she chooses to remember.

I'm dramatic, my mom says. Make a big deal out of nothing.

Her memoir would be full of PTO meetings and snow cone days, and raising money to buy a marquee for the school. Not racking up charges on all the credit cards to buy us brand name clothes at department stores. Not spending money without looking at prices, hiding receipts and saying, Don't tell Dad. Like he didn't know. Mom would not write a memoir about Dad losing his job and that, due to our maxed-out credit cards and mounting debt, that our family was forced to go bankrupt and lose our possessions. Mom would not write that after my twelfth year, I disappeared from my family, and never came back. I was a ghost inside our home, and what happens to the invisible one? They are sought out by those looking for game.

Names

Angel. Baby. Honey. Lester. Baby. Tiny One. Brat. Stupid. So smart. Write a story. Write a play. So smart. Shut up, stupid. Go away. Go to sleep. Find someone else. Las Chicas or Las Rucas. La Shy Girl. Nerd. So smart for a girl, a Mexican. Ain't got no friends. Homeless and trashy. Skeleton. Boney. Huesos. Bag of bones. Skeletor. The ugly one. Skinny skeleton. Anorexic. Littles. Bit. Little bit. Baby. Hot. Rape girl. Tramp. Slut. His bitch. Bitch. Her bitch. Stupid bitch. Gangster. Trash. Thug. Dyke. Lesbian. Part of the whore chore dancers. Mexican trash. Mexican whore. White girl. Wanna be white girl. Snob. Conceited. Loser. Loner. Girl-who-eats-lunch-in-bathroom. Girl who got herself raped. Idiot. Ghetto. Gifted. Nobody. Loose. Fast. As dumb as a monkey. Dick sucker. Nothing. I don't want you. Beautiful. Artist. So smart. So talented. Writer. You should write. Evil. Aggressive. Defensive. Troublemaker. Hot wire. Crazy. Friend. Dear. Momma. Baby. Love. I need you to hold me. Momma. I loved what you wrote. Crazy. Sick all the time. I hope you and your children die. Here's a list of the things you have done wrong. Goodbye. I need to talk to you. You're nothing like her. You're a good mom. You're a good mom, Momma. I love you more than all the universes. I love you. Good night, Momma. Sweet dreams. I hope you feel better, Momma. Momma, momma, can I show you now? Poet. My neighbor. Woman on the corner. Professor. Did you see her? Disabled. Frail. Forceful. Gaunt. Unhealthy. Does she look unhealthy? Takes no crap. Baby. Momma. Tiny one. Beauty. Miss. I miss you. Cruel. Kind. Loving. Loved. Hated. Open. You don't get to say. I'm so glad to see your face.

Supermoon

That first night of camping we saw a supermoon as we walked back to our tents to get ready for bedtime.

I was 14 years old laying on a large stretch of granite rock in a primitive area of Enchanted Rock, a state park in Texas near Fredericksburg, and next to me lay my dearest friend, D, whose father had just died from cancer a month before.

It was not something I would normally do, or think of investigating doing, and there I was, hiking and carrying a large backpack, then laying on a large stretch of granite rock next to my friend under the light of a supermoon, the first one I ever saw.

It was at night that I felt overcome with being a person amid all the natural beauty—a vast collection of stars and black space and the soothing sounds of night animals and insects which I realized my whole life had been filtered out by the hum and blaze of streetlights, late night basketball games, trucks buzzing on the major road behind our neighborhood, everything else.

It seemed impossible for the moon to be spectacularly round, a perfect, orange-tinged oval, a shelter, just as it seemed impossible that D's father had just died from cancer a month before.

We lay under the nighttime sky where it was dark enough to see so many stars I began to feel dizzy by the sheer enormity, its endlessness. Then a comet would flicker in the light of one of the arms of the Milky Way, and things seemed more manageable, more full of shape, and I would fall into feeling calm again. But not D. That first night, she must have felt the same thing, a panic at how large and full the night sky seemed, how oblivious it was to her loss, but she did not find her way to peace. She bolted up and ran back to the campsite, shaking her head in disbelief.

Was it any wonder that D and I could not be human to each other except here? I held her hand in the dark and listened to her as she said her father would never be coming back, as if she realized it for the first time, or considered the thought as a something to absorb as fact.

My own parents at home were always struggling—my dad with a recent bankruptcy and my mom with the realization that she had no plans for herself and revolved her life around my activities like a cheerleader.

They must have felt this weight all along, and maybe this was why they seemed distracted driving me to and from school and activities or my job at the mail place or my job at the food court. They had to have seen this type of sky, these types of trees and shrub. And for some reason we couldn't live in it, and be a part of it, and they did the best they could with what was available to them. I considered that they might have tried the best they could.

Hike

We hitched our backpacks onto our shoulders and back, tying it around our chest and waist. It had everything we needed for three days to venture into a primitive part of the state park.

It was 90 degrees and the sun had started heating the rocky trail so that it glowed in a heavy stupor.

The locusts and flies swarmed above shrub and blackjack and post oaks as we stood at the bottom of the rocky slope. I looked at the trail we planned to climb, straining under the weight of my pack and already feeling tired.

The neighborhood I'd spent my childhood, Greenfield Village, named after English pastoral scenes that I read about in Victorian literature, did not have grass that swayed in a moor's blustery wind, nor trees that one could sit under to read a book in its shade.

Our neighborhood, as were all the surrounding neighborhoods that I was familiar with where my friends or family lived, were similar; lower middle-class tract houses of four repeating designs, set on lots with a small front lawn and a small backyard, both covered in hard St. Augustine grass that yellowed in early spring.

Sometimes there was hardy shrubbery, or like our yard, a row of monkey grass protecting a tidy family of perennials.

Behind our street, beyond our back fence, was the thin stream of Greens bayou, wild with weeds and tall grass and swarming with mosquitos and grasshoppers, and unkempt enough to let us hear a chorus of grasshoppers at night chirping.

I did not miss what I didn't know, what had once been swamp life, a verdant and lush landscape of the bayou South, now bulldozed and filled in with concrete to create this new middle-class neighborhood for the upwardly mobile Mexican American, Black and Asian families, so we could reach closer to the American Dream. It never occurred to me that we lived among a lack of trees, flowers, vegetation, a natural environment.

The heat and the sun, notoriously harsh in South Texas, didn't bother me either, even in the summer. The neighborhood children and I played all day long in the street or the yard until my knees turned dark brown and we came inside only to eat or drink or go to sleep.

Our neighborhood bordered a large highway, with major streets full of strip malls that had the grocery stores, department stores, dollar and drug stores that allowed us to not have to drive very far. Going into town was both unnecessary and expensive, and was done once or twice a year for us, although my father rode the bus downtown every day for work, which took at least 45 minutes each way.

*

Once my father got lost when our family drove to an event inside the city limits, and we passed an area with enormous spreading oak trees that reached their limbs over streets like wind-blown hair, swan necks leaning over in rows of green and shadow.

I saw it briefly as we drove by, and my father shouted as we drove by a gate that we were passing a great university, a place that very few people attended except the extremely intelligent and wealthy.

It was just a flash of an image, but that leafy shade, the promise held in its limbs with a connection to nature I never knew was missing, it filled me with a knowledge of something that I wanted, something we didn't have.

The image of those trees became one filled with longing and it was enough to feed a fantasy of escape, one that formed the trajectory of my adult life.

When we were driving through the city, my mom told me that there are areas of Houston she remembers as undeveloped, riding a horse through and seeing only wild land. She recalls eating ripe tomatoes from her uncle's farm, how the juice would just run down her chin in the back of a pickup with all her cousins. She remembers that beloved uncle teaching her how to graft plants, how to make a plant into a shrub, how much to water and when to stop watering a garden.

She watches a lot of television in her room after work saying she deserves rest, her feet propped up and pillows around her head.

When I remember these stories, I try to imagine her small child's body bumping along a dirt road with miles of nothing but grassland and shrub. I liked to imagine her happiness there in that place, for although she was an orphan and had a difficult home life and was often beaten, it must have made her feel part of the world, a child with a home.

Chemo

D's father was dying. Last night she'd said that there were clumps of his hair coming out in the faucet, and that he was pale and weak from the chemotherapy. He'd had to take time off from his job at the metal factory where he was a machinist and often worked overtime to provide D and her brother and mother with "extras," like trips to Sea World, or for his only daughter, the latest designer purse and shoes.

So, I said nothing when she insulted my body, called me ugly or boney. I just smiled to show I was unaffected. I'd never had a serious boyfriend and the boy from the baseball team she'd recently set me up with, who'd I'd gone out with on one date, had stopped answering my calls after a week. He'd been coming to my locker every day, waiting to say hi, then disappeared after I didn't have sex with him.

That fall of freshmen year, he'd taken me to a huge party of his baseball friends, the first high school party I'd ever been to, and I stood off in the corner staring as everyone, people I barely knew, got trashed and wasted or made out in the backyard. I'd clearly lost some standing with him.

He'd gone to get something from a friend, and, when he came back after far too long, we went into his friend's car to make out. I saw people staring through the window, so I sat up. I was on display as if to see who'd won a bet. Suddenly, his absence, lack of consideration and my naivete reached a boiling point.

Take me home, I said.

*

When Thomas first came to say hi to me, he was in his baseball uniform and his long bangs were slick with sweat. I was putting books in my locker, then methodically checking my folder to see what homework I had and then what books I needed to take back out.

Immediately, my face burned hot and flushed red, and I wondered how small and frail my body looked in the new jeans my dad had gotten me, the smallest he could find at the discount department store we shopped at. That morning, I'd tied a belt on to keep them up, a belt I'd already poked several holes in to make it fit my frame.

I put on a shirt that both hid my cinched waist and hopefully didn't make my small chest appear sunken or unattractive. My face was nice when I wanted it to be, D had said. In the bathroom that morning, she lit a match to a mascara stick to melt the makeup and outlined my eyes in black. Now, see, she said. Not so bad. Thanks to me.

*

Here, at Enchanted Rock, none of that existed. We woke up and went out of our tents to clean up and help make breakfast, and the only preening we did was to move sticks or limbs out of our pathway.

We were four girls, ages 13 to 14 years old, with a troop leader who must have been about 40 and who based her lifestyle on abstinences of every kind. At first, I didn't believe her daughter when she'd said she'd never seen television or listened to the radio because they had neither in their house.

We drank lots of water, we sang and fought, we stooped to watch lizards and snakes and examine wildflowers, lichen and gayfeather, and the leader taught us how the long stretches of cracked granite walk we tread on was made from hardened magma. D and I put our feet in the cool water of a small vernal pool where the rocks were sharp and uneven.

The Drill

In high school, I knew the drill. D was friends with everyone, though, in private, girls said they hated her and boys said they just wanted to fuck her. There was never an exception.

After she'd introduce me with some nickname-approximate-to-fag, I'd straighten my back and say the cruelest thing I could imagine, but as if it were a joke, for instance, "At least my mom can see her own ankles and doesn't look like a linebacker, and seeing how y'all look alike, we know your fate" or "Fag who? Seems like you're anxious if you don't look in the mirror at least two times minute and that you'd rather just fuck yourself."

And D would laugh and say, "See! This girl is hilarious!"

My repertoire went beyond the insulting and profane, some of which was too smart or referential (for highschoolers) to understand.

"Fate? Anxious?" one guy had said in one such incident, mocking my vocabulary. "What is this friend of yours? Some nerd? This girl is fucking weird as shit."

*

Soon, I only ate lunch with her, which was difficult in a class of almost 750, but she was fast in eliminating new friends I had, and getting rid of the old ones, with my complicity. When no other people were around, she didn't need to perform as much. She was a friend, I thought, because we began to share what happened to us, even though, deep down, I knew she could and would squash me if she needed to.

Though sought after as an ally and envied by girls, and followed by salivating boys and even teachers, D was not popular. Everyone said they knew her, everyone said they'd spent time with her in one way or another, but almost no one knew what happened in her house. I did.

We tried to save each other—and we failed. D was the one person, in secret, telling me I was beautiful, smart, funny, talented, a sister, her soul mate. Each of us faced our teen years of self-destruction and severe depression by loving each other in the only twisted way we knew how.

*

D and I were dysfunctional, but we shared an intimacy that was all-consuming, one that pervaded our cells. Our minds nearly open and bare to each other. Through our trauma and shared history, our relationship made us both monstrous and saviors to each other, all of it constructed around our secret thoughts and desires and machinations, real or imagined.

At 20, I found myself lost...in a prestigious, wooded campus surrounded by students who had been valedictorian of their well-to-do high schools. There was no one there who could understand me, I thought, not even myself, and especially not without D.

I felt foreign, unsophisticated, and utterly alone.
I left her anyway.

Strike

As a child, I kept pet gerbils in my bedroom. One year, I had a female gerbil that kept eating her newborn litters. I would go to sleep with the aquarium at the foot of my bed, hearing her tiny scurries in the straw as she prepared to give birth. I'd wake up and see her slumped stomach, licking her paws, or fast asleep, curled in a tight ball of herself, the babies nowhere to be found. The last time she gave birth, I walked in to find the hairless curled bodies next to her, so vulnerable in their translucent skin that I could hardly look at them. I placed the newborns in a green Tupperware bowl, thinking this time I would save them.

In the morning, I went straight to their bowl in my closet. Their tiny claws were folded in loose fists, every single one now dead. I was six and didn't understand that the newborns needed to be both separated and fed; I just thought I was saving them from their mother. I never asked for another gerbil again, and when the adults died, I didn't mourn them. I always remembered the babies the mother didn't want, the

ones it hurt for me to look at. I buried them in the backyard
and marked their grave with wildflowers and a collection of
clay-colored pebbles.

*

In the summer of 2016, I returned from a family trip after
a week of sun and swimming, nights on the lawn at our hotel
watching movies on a large outdoor screen. All through the trip
and especially after our return I am conscious of a deep, un-
shakeable sickness, like a very bad flu.

When we arrive home, I sleep and sleep. One morning, I
hear the baby cry and put my feet down on the side of the bed
to stand and walk to him. My left leg is weak and my foot drags.
I go to him and realize I am weaker as I pull him out of his crib.

My daughters, aged seven and four, start school. I pick out
their clothes; pack their lunches every morning. They come
home with hand-outs and I hold them close to my face, then
far away—I am having trouble reading the letters. I am having
trouble seeing the computer screen. I am walking with a full
limp. There is pain blooming behind one eye, sometimes two.
Do you have a black eye? my second grader asks one day. I
always wear sunglasses now, because of the pain.

Should I buy a cane? I ask my doctor. She shrugs. If it helps.

For a period of time from 2016 to 2017, the doctors order four MRIs, a lumbar puncture, dozens and dozens of blood tests, eye scans, images of the nerves in the eyes, nerve conduction tests. My symptoms, meanwhile, come and go. There is no diagnosis, no name for what my body does—only descriptions; medications; the decision to rest or ask for help, use a cane, wear an ice-pack vest to lower my body temperature, as the sun and humidity make my body shut down. The symptoms are similar to multiple sclerosis, but there is not enough evidence to diagnose it.

*

Sometimes I whisk through whole days in complete health. I can do yoga poses in my living room, one leg in the air. I twist sideways, I balance, I reach.

Sometimes I fall while walking slowly on the treadmill or have a day when everything I hold seems to slip easily from my hands.

Then there are days when I wake up and realize that, overnight, some new symptom has set in.

Days I can't use my muscles to write, days I can't control the muscles to speak as well as the day before.

*

This is what I have learned from the past months of unexplained illness and pain: We are made of equal parts death and life, more or less.

Some people's experiences tip the scale toward that darker matter.

These are people we seek to avoid, whose mere presence reminds us in the aisle of the grocery store, at the children's birthday party, at dinner with friends, at school events, that what we most fear and want to deny can be embodied in a person's physical form. The human equivalent of those newborn gerbils, so achingly bare that it is painful to look at them. We don't know how to save them.

This is what I make of the gymnastics teacher who sees me on a bad day, when I can barely walk and am using the cane as a leg. She is the one who taught both my daughters how to flip over a beam, using their arms like two strong mini poles, swinging their bodies in the air. She is so upset she cannot speak to me, and babbles incomprehensibly. She is still babbling when I take my daughter's hand and walk away.

*

We are taught to exalt the body in motion: the perfect limbs, balance, coordination, and grace dancing across an endless football field.

*

A man who has been accused of sexual assault, a man who speaks of women as if they are his mules, a man who ridiculed a reporter with a physical disability, was then the president of the United States.

The day he is elected, I barely manage to walk from my car to the elevator at the rheumatologist's office.

You need a brain biopsy, she says to me. And you need chemo meds.

I am still digesting this as I drag myself back to the van parked in a space that would have felt close, unremarkable, just six months ago.

Today the space I have to travel to get to the van reminds me of my body's condition. With every step, I think people are staring.

I drive home carefully, worried that I might haven an accident even though the doctor has said I'm okay to drive. My thoughts wander. I think of the arm movements of the disabled journalist, the one the then-candidate emulated. He was doing something else, a Republican friend messages me. It's not what you say it is. I think of all the words the president has used with intent to strip down, bury, or erase people; I think of all the words I've heard in the mouths of many others, mostly men and boys.

*

I am in a space where wetback also means whore which also means cripple. All different words, all meant to dissolve power. What will I let it do to me?

*

What is wrong with you? What is wrong with you? Every day, teachers, friends, strangers, readers at my book events, ask me or tell me what is wrong with me. I know what you should do.

What did you do to yourself? Maybe it's allergies. Maybe it's mental illness.

During flares, my body can be disconcerting to others. It is seen as a body that needs immediate holistic treatment, aligned Chakras, and Jesus.

Have you talked to your psychiatrist about this? a friend asks me on the phone.

Are you stressed before this happens, or after? Is this because of stress?

There are so many versions of the question, with the underlying demand, unspoken: Tell me how this is not real, how you made it up in your sick mind.

Who do I remind you of? I think, when other people are busy talking about my body.

I am not believed that my body's disease is not my fault.
I don't blame them for wanting to look away. It is hard to

miss that spread-eagled jump of youth, to consider that we might come crashing down at any moment. Thank you, I say to them. I know you want to help.

I turn, walk away, hang up on them.

Learning to Swim

My father put me on his back, held onto my legs, and went underwater with me in the neighborhood swimming pool. There was the flash of the June sun becoming brighter and then disappearing into a dark haze.

I was five years old, had never put my head under the water, and didn't know how to let out air like a swimmer, how to hold my breath properly underwater.

I started drowning.

I began to struggle under the water. I tried to pull my legs and arms out of his grip.

Out of protection, my father held me tighter. He continued diving under and out of the water again, and again, not realizing I would not instinctively hold my breath or blow out air. I opened my mouth to scream and kept swallowing water. Under the surface, here was the muffle of my muted scream, the hush of the blue chlorinated world that I was sure was going to drown me.

I remember the sound of the teenagers at the pool, their

splashing and yelling as they tried to hold each other's heads under the water. Some were holding a somersault contest. Others were daring each other to jump into the deep end.

*

Then we were above again, and on top of the neighborhood kids' noise was my own sharp inhale of air and the pumping of my heart in my ears.

When my dad carried me out of the pool, he was confused by my violent coughing. So many of the children in our neighborhood learned to swim from friends or by being thrown in the water, when instinct that I couldn't understand kicked in.

My father learned from free swim lessons at the YMCA in the 1950s with his siblings, on the days when Mexican and Blacks were allowed to use the pool.

I never took swim lessons as a child. There was only enough money, barely, to send my two older siblings to a couple of lessons in the summer. I felt content in my comfortable, dry spot on a bench or at the edge of the pool as I watched my brother and sister jump into the water as if it were the most natural thing for a person to do.

From my earliest memories, I have been afraid of water, the lack of control I felt when I was submerged in it.

I spent my whole childhood and early adulthood in Houston pools and swim parks carefully managing to keep my head above water, my hair always dry as I stayed in the shallow end.

I envied the freedom I saw in the young people around me who could jump into the deep end headlong, their bodies welcoming the cold shock of water as it took them into a hushed space.

However, the second I felt myself close to being swallowed by water, the depth of a pool or sea gaping below me into dark blue, a terrible panic rose through my body.

The fear was so palpable that the sea, even to this day, is a personal symbol of ominousness, a large mouth trying to swallow the world.

*

At 24, on our honeymoon to the Yucatan, I went snorkeling with my husband far out in the Pacific Ocean, with a guide that took us by a small motor-powered boat.

I felt the need to be daring, to leave childish fears behind that surely I could control by now. I had earned the right to not be afraid.

Wearing a bright orange life vest, once in the water, my body began to sink inside its puffy shape. The waves, which had looked merely lapping before, were forceful and choppy.

How big the waves really were, the fact that I still couldn't swim—the old fear rose up in me, panic in my throat.

I watched my husband swim away from me.

I began beating the water back with my arms and my legs. Still every time a wave reached me, I swallowed gulps of salt water. I had forgotten about my snorkeling gear; it was a nuisance on my head as I panicked and it had floated away.

The guide looked back and saw me struggling. He swam to me, lithe and liquid like a dolphin, carried me back to the boat.

*

It was summer when my daughter was born. There was something terrifying in how she depended on me, especially during the night when I was afraid that I would sleep so deeply she would surely go hungry.

She turned a year when I decided it was time for me to learn how to swim. She was walking and the world was so much larger than her, seemed like it might hurt her at any minute. When we took her to the pool in her baby-sized swimsuit, trimmed with ruffles, she seemed to enjoy it, splashing in the water and kicking her feet.

But I imagined her falling into a pool by accident. She was frightened even when I washed her hair and the water poured into her eyes. And if we held her too close to the pool's surface, her eyes grew big and terrified.

She must learn to swim, I thought. And because she did, I

had to as well, in order to help her. I couldn't stand the fear in her eyes, that she couldn't do something when I knew it could be learned.

In my first swim lesson at the Jewish Community Center near my house, my private swim teacher, gentle and without judgment, simply had me put my face in the water.

I did this repeatedly for an hour. My heart seized in my chest, and then relaxed, along with the practice. I'm going to drown, I wanted to tell her. So many times, I thought, I'll just do it one more time.

You are buoyant. Your body is full of air. It can't drown if you don't let it, she told me. But you have to relax.

She was holding me under my arms as I floated on my back. It was a struggle for me to allow my head to relax into the water. I was breathing quickly as I willed my legs to not thrash, my arms not to push against her. I thought of how I held my daughter in her own swim lessons, how I tried to show her what her body could do.

It was not with words that I learned over the course of several months how to swim, albeit adequately and slow-paced. I just kept going back to the water. Like entering a mikvah, the ritual Jewish bath, I stepped into the water with the anticipation of transforming by body, with the same sense of shock and of the water's powerful presence; I entered anticipating the body's same acclimation to its temperature.

Every time was still a struggle, but what I struggled against each time was different.

First, it was the fear of water on my face, the discomfort of it.

Then it was the panic of being under water, that my body would forget how to blow out air and instead suck in the water despite my willing it not to.

Later, it was that my arms would grow tired and weak and I would be stranded in the deep end by my own body, sinking down into failure.

I kept going back. I broke my wrist and I practiced with a waterproof cast. I began going more frequently, several times a week. The fear became familiar, not welcome, but part of the process of my body's reaction to swimming. I used it.

*

At night, I read the biography of an American long-distance swimmer, Lynn Cox, whose book *Swimming to Antarctica* tells the story of how she faced sub-freezing temperatures in a daring swim.

She was also, often, filled with fear, despite her training. And yet, she broke records, even at an early age, and continued to swim. She welcomed the disorienting atmosphere of swimming at night, making it part of her practice.

*

On my last lesson that summer, I stood at the edge of the pool near the deep end. I am five feet, one inch. I looked down at my teacher, who was wearing what she always wore at our lessons: a black t-shirt, swim shorts, a black cap, and tennis shoes to protect her feet from being scratched up against the pool as she pulled bodies and turned arms and legs.

She looked at me, said Bend low.

I jumped. The sun was brighter that day, hotter. I didn't feel it. Instead, I felt my body in the air, its weight as it carried me down. I sank into the water, felt the cover of water above me, my teacher a black blur as I looked at her through my goggles. I felt like I had won something, a gift I gave to myself.

Afterward, I swam the whole length of the Olympic-sized pool by myself. I struggled, I spat out water, my arms and legs were not graceful like the videos I'd watched of professional swimmers.

Then I did it again. And again.

It was as if I was reaching for something, instead of escaping.

Because, initially, I had started learning to swim for my daughter, to protect her.

I borrowed fear and let it guide my body, let it struggle without giving up. My mind had done that for years, in some ways.

Now my body, finally, was catching up.

NOTES AND ACKNOWLEDGEMENTS

From *The Popol Vuh: A New English Version*, translated by Michael Bazzett. Copyright © 2018 by Michael Bazzett. Reprinted with the permission of The Permissions Company, LLC on behalf of Milkweed Editions. milkweed.org.

Xibalba refers to the underworld, the place of the Death Lords, where the heroes of *The Popol Vuh* defeat death.

Thank you to the following publications in which essays or parts of essays appeared: *Catapult, The Houston Chronicle, Raising Mothers, Southwest: The Magazine,* and *Texas Review.*

My love and gratitude for the support and care I received while writing this book from the following people: Michael and my children; my brother Russell; Lisa, Jaclyn, and Lucy; writing friends and family Jenn Givhan and Benjamin Garcia; and to all the faculty and students at the Alma College MFA program in creative writing.

ABOUT THE AUTHOR

Leslie Contreras Schwartz is a multi-genre writer, a 2021 Academy of American Poets Laureate Fellow, and the 2019-2021 Houston Poet Laureate. She is the winner of the C&R Press 2022 Nonfiction Prize for *From the Womb of Sky and Earth*, an. She is the author of five collections of poetry, including *The Body Cosmos* (Mouthfeel Press, forthcoming); *Black Dove / Paloma Negra* (FlowerSong Press, 2020), a finalist for 2020 Best Book of Poetry from the Texas Institute of Letters; and *Nightbloom & Cenote* (St. Julian Press, 2018), a semi-finalist for the 2017 Tupelo Press Dorset Prize, judged by Ilya Kaminsky. Her work has appeared in *AGNI, Catapult, EPOCH, Gulf Coast, Gulf Coast, Missouri Review, Pleiades, Zocalo Public Square*, and the anthology *Houston Noir* (Akashic Books, 2019), as well as 2019 *The Best Small Fiction* anthology. Recent work has been featured with on Academy of American Poets *Poem-A-Day* and the Poetry Foundation. She has collaborated or been commissioned for community poetry projects with the Academy of American Poets, the City of Houston, the Houston Grand Opera, and The Moody Center of the Arts at Rice University. Contreras Schwartz is currently a poetry and nonfiction faculty member at Alma College's MFA low-residency program in creative writing, and a lecturer in creative writing at Rice University. She is a graduate of The Program for Writers at Warren Wilson College and earned a bachelor's at Rice University. For more on her work, visit lesliecschwartz.com.

Leslie Contreras Schwartz

C&R PRESS TITLES

NONFICTION

From the Womb of Sky and Earth by Leslie Contreras Schwartz
This is Infertility by Kirsten McLennan
Curriculum Vitae by Gregory de la Haba
Many Paths by Bruce McEver
By the Bridge or By the River by Amy Roma
Gatbsy's Child by Dorin Schumacher
Credo by Rita Banerjee and Diana Norma Szokolyai
Women in the Literary Landscape by Doris Weatherford, et al

FICTION

Transcendent Gardening by Ed Falco
Juniper Street by Joan Frank
All I Should Not Tell by Brian Leung
A History of the Cat by Anis Shivani
Pages from the Textbook of an Alternate History
            by Phong Nguyen
No Good, Very Bad Asian by Lelund Cheuk
Last Tower to Heaven by Jacob Paul
Surrendering Appomattox by Jacob M. Appel
Headlong by Ron MacLean
A Diet of Worms by Erik Rasmussen

The Pleasures of Queuing by Erik Martiny
Life During Wartime by Katie Rogin
Cloud Diary by Steve Mitchell
Ivy vs. Dogg by Brian Leung
While You Were Gone by Sybil Baker
Made by Mary by Laura Catherine Brown
Spectrum by Martin Ott
That Man in Our Lives by Xu Xi

SHORT FICTION

A Mother's Tale & Other Stories by Khanh Ha
Fathers of Cambodian Time-Travel Science by Bradley Bazzle
Two Californias by Robert Glick
Meditations on the Mother Tongue by An Tran
The Protester Has Been Released by Janet Sarbanes

ESSAY AND CREATIVE NONFICTION

In the Room of Persistent Sorry by Kristina Marie Darling
the internet is for real by Chris Campanioni
Je suis l'autre by Kristina Marie Darling
Immigration Essays by Sybil Baker
Death of Art by Chris Campanioni

POETRY

Curare by Lucian Mattison
Leaving the Skin on the Bear by Kelli Allen
How to Kill Youself Instead of Your Children
        byQuincy Scott Jones
Lottery of Inimacies by Jonathan Katz
What Feels Like Love by Tom C. Hunley
The Rented Altar by Lauren Berry
Communicatingroups by Stu Watson
Between the EArth and Sky by Eleanor Kedney
What Need Have We for Such as We by Amanda Auerbach
Give a Girl Chaos by Heidi Seaborn
The Miracles by Amy Lemmon
Banjo's Inside Coyote by Kelli Allen
A Family is a House by Dustin Pearson
Millenial Roost by Dustin Pearson
Objects in Motion by Jonathan Katz
My Stunt Double by Travis Denton
Dark Horse by Kristina Marie Darling
Lessons in Camoflauge by Martin Ott
Notes to the Beloved by Michelle Bitting
Negro Side of the Moon by Earl Braggs
Ex Domestica by E.G. Cunningham
All My Heroes are Broke by Ariel Francisco
Like Lesser Gods by Bruce McEver
Les Fauves by Barbara Crooker

Imagine Not Drowning by Kelli Allen
Tall as You are Tall Between Them by Annie Christain
Free Boat: Collected Lies and Love Poems by John Reed
The Couple Who Fell to Earth by Michelle Bitting

ART

East Village Closed by Billy the Artist
Things You Don't Here Twice by Billy the Artist
Casanova Erotica by Sonia Hensler

Printed in the USA
CPSIA information can be obtained
at www.ICGtesting.com
LVHW091103081124
795983LV00006B/1489

* 9 7 8 1 9 4 9 5 4 0 4 3 7 *